The Lost Art of Initial Messaging

My Guide to Initial Messages While Online Dating

S.W. Campbell

Published by Shawn Campbell

The Lost Art of Initial Messaging

The Lost Art of Initial Messaging

ISBN: 979-8-9870287-4-2

For all of those who never give up the hope.

Also for Jeff, thanks for all the Jeff Maps.

The Lost Art of Initial Messaging

Introduction

A long time ago, before online dating morphed into the swiping assembly line that it is today, online dating was kind of different. Where today you have a couple of photos and a few fun fact blurbs which nobody reads, back in the dark ages of the early 2010s online dating involved a complete download of yourself into an online dating profile. At the time, the average profile would include albums of photos, the equivalent of several full-length essays describing who the person was and what they wanted, and answers to possibly hundreds of prepared questions ranging from political views to lifestyle preferences, to a quite detailed list of sexual proclivities.

To say the profiles of yesteryear were extensive would be an understatement. Were you looking for a political moderate, who wanted to have kids, liked paragliding, didn't believe in climate change, and was into light bondage? Well, you could find them. It was amazing what people would put on their profiles, things that they would likely never tell friends or family, and most certainly not random strangers met in bars and other such in real life meetup points. However, all was plastered freely on a website owned by some private corporation for anyone willing to set up an account to peruse at their leisure. Given all this oversharing, it will probably come as a bit of a surprise to those of you who did not live through this strange phenomenon that the only thing that wasn't freely shared was the person's name. You could see them in a bikini, read their life goals, and know their fetishes, but a given name was apparently one step too far. Amongst it all we all somehow clung to the rather shaky belief that a profile name somehow protected our anonymity. Oh, what a time to be alive.

I crawled into the morass of online dating in 2011. I was in my late twenties and having largely squeezed dry the possibilities of friends of friends and those still single and involved in the same activities, and not really being all that good at chatting up random strangers, I decided to broaden my world and throw my hat into the online ring. After spending the requisite week setting up my profile, I selected the profile name *Don't_Panic*, an alias whose advice was more pointed towards myself than possible dates, and jumped headlong into the massive endeavor before me.

I should probably state from the start that I am neither what one would call traditionally charming nor handsome. It's not that I'm a troll who just yells 'wanna smush' at women or anything like that, but I'm also not the type of person who gets undue attention from the fairer sex based purely on my looks and my mastery of the art of seduction. After all, if I was that kind of person, I probably wouldn't be online dating. At least that was my mindset at the time, online dating not yet being the universal way of life which it later became. It's for this reason that before I even got started, I decided on a couple of rules regarding the writing of an initial message.

For those of us who aren't drop dead gorgeous, the initial message represented our one chance to get our foot in the door. It was a bit of a crapshoot. There were no matches or anything of that nature. No, you just picked a random person and sent them a message, hoping for the best. As a result, a woman might receive hundreds of messages in any given week. If an average guy like me stood any chance of standing out in this crowd, I'd have to make a good first impression. Not being a complete moron, I figured that the way of doing this would be similar to how it was done in real life. It was a balancing act. One wanted to be funny, but not overly weird, and one needed to show that they were interested in a potential mate for specific reasons, but not in a creepy stalkerish way. What follows are the initial messages I sent out over the next several years, unedited and in all their glory.

Attempt #1
12Birds29

Background:

The sheer scale of online dating at the time was completely overwhelming. Oh sure, there are more people than ever online dating today, but back then people were putting a lot more information out there, and unless you were ridiculously good looking, you damn well better be able to show that you did some reading before sending out a message. Oh sure, I of course based my initial filter on whether or not I found the other person attractive, but after that it was at minimum fifteen minutes of reading their profile before spending even more time crafting a brilliant initial message, which might not even get read by someone, either because they did not find me attractive for some reason or because the sheer volume of options made going through all of them an excruciating chore. In other words, it was a lot of effort for what amounted to a complete shot in the dark.

The first time is always the hardest. You really have no idea what you're doing, but you try your damndest to keep anyone from knowing it. The first profile I picked was that of a woman calling herself 12Birds29, who judging by her pictures and word choice was some kind of an artist. Here's a woman, I thought, who would understand my sensitive side. Someone who looked at the world and described it in the magical terms that were slipping away from me, eroded by a growing post-adolescence pessimism. Seeing no reason to beat around the bush, I just put it all out there for her to see.

The Message:

I've always found people with artistic skills fascinating. It's probably because no matter how hard I try I've never had the skill to create in any medium what I see in my head, which I find frustrating. I have however, slowly over time taught myself to take photos, mostly landscapes, and have had some some people complement my them. Though my photos seem more like recognizing an opportunity when I see it rather then any kind of artistic talent.

I'd like to say up front that I really don't feel like my profle represents me as well as it could, though I'm not entirely sure how to correct this, yet. There's a lot of different facets to me and it takes time to reveal all of them.

All that being said I'm sending this because you seem like you'd be an interesting person to talk to and get to know. I imagine you get a lot of messages so I should probably write something enticing or witty, but I'm fairly tired right now and nothing is coming to mind. I could probably force something, but it would mostly just be bullshit.

Anyways, if you have any interest in getting to know me better, message me back.

P.S. How far can a dog run into the woods?

The Result:

Okay, now imagine you're sitting at a bar, having a nice drink or something, and some random asshat comes up and says all of the above to you? How are you going to react? I'm not really sure what I was thinking, especially with the riddle at the end, and that's not even going into the fact that I'm apparently terrible at spelling and grammar. The whole message makes me cringe to this day when I read it. But then again, perhaps I'm wrong about the whole situation. Perhaps 12Birds29 never got back to me because her mind was too absorbed by the convoluted twists and turns of my riddle. Yeah, that was probably it.

Also, for those of you who are wondering, a dog can run halfway into the woods. After that it is running out.

Attempt #2
ChemicalKat

Background:

All right, the first time didn't go so well. Obviously, there was room for improvement. For example, it would probably help if I brought up some things to possibly talk about. Maybe something from their profile, you know, so they would know I had actually bothered to read it. Also, it probably wouldn't hurt to do some proofreading before sending the message out. It sure as hell couldn't hurt. So the quest began again. I sifted through countless profiles to find someone who looked interesting, hunting desperately for something which might light a loquacious spark. Flying cars! ChemicalKat's profile included a snide remark about the lack of flying cars!

The Message:

I am severely disappointed in the total lack of flying cars. I feel like this is something we were promised the 21st century would have, and that science and industry just let us down. Don't get me wrong, I do love many of our achievements, but c'mon, flying cars.

One of my favorite book series is the Mars Trilogy by Kim Stanley Robinson which outlines the colonization and terraforming of Mars. If I had a chance to join some kind of Mars colonization effort, I would do it in a heartbeat. Keeping my fingers crossed on that one.

The Result:

At the time, it seemed like such an obvious step from one to the other. Flying cars belong to the world of science fiction, so why not mention my favorite science fiction series? I'll tell you why, because it feels disjointed as hell when reading over it again. It's kind of like if someone brought up something you wanted to talk about, and then brought up a completely different topic before you could even answer. As you can probably guess, I didn't hear anything back.

Attempt #3
RosewaterLips

Background:

Sometimes profiles have a strong pull in the physical department, if you know what I mean (insert winky face here), but upon reading them they raise all sorts of red flags. At first you try to excuse it with the idea that they probably just have a weird sense of humor, but that nagging feeling doesn't go away. I don't know, the whole thing is pretty damn subjective. Such is the dilemma I had upon reading RosewasterLips' profile, which proudly proclaimed that first, she wasn't on meth or something, second, she would only date someone who could tread water longer than her, and third, she was a badass knitter. Okay, let's be honest with each other, it wasn't really a dilemma. I'm pretty weird myself, so I shouldn't really judge. Plus, she was pretty damn hot.

The Message:

Congratulations for not being on meth or something. That overall seems like a positive.

I can tread water for 30 minutes, would this be long enough to be competitive or should I start some kind of water treading training program with a Rockyesque montage?

Also, knitting is pretty good, but crocheting is more bad ass. Not judging, just saying.

The Result:

Believe it or not, the above message worked, which may or may not have been a red flag in and of itself. The online dating world, much like the real world, is strange in that you never know what attracts you to another person. However, also much like the real world, sometimes the rocket engines light, but nothing happens. Though RosewaterLips and I messaged back and forth a few times, she soon after disappeared back into the electronic ether. Vanishing in all but my mind where she treads water and knits forever. But on the plus side, I had gotten a response after only three attempts, which was pretty good for the old ego. Convinced it would only be a matter of time, I ventured forth once again.

Attempt #4
FoxyHound32

Background:

Sometimes there's a profile that just doesn't have much of a hook. Either they haven't written that much, there just isn't anything to latch onto, or perhaps you're just getting lazy. Up until this point, I had simply moved past these profiles, figuring someone with a half-ass profile would probably just half-ass their way through most things in life. However, with this one, for some reason, which totally didn't have anything to do with how attractive she was, I decided to throw out an equally inadequate piece of bait on the off chance that somebody calling themselves FoxyHound32 might bite.

The Message:

This is probably a horrible way to start a conversation, but I'm wondering what makes your dog so special and unique? Looks like your everyday Aussie Shepherd/Blue Heeler mix to me.

The Result:

I never got to find out what made that damn dog so special. My bait must have not been that good, because FoxyHound32 swam by without even a nibble. Looking back, it probably wasn't the best idea to start off by putting someone on the defensive, especially if the topic was their dog, which judging by how she went on and on about it in her profile she would have probably married it if such things were legal.

Attempt #5
Dinomite69

Background:

The profile of the woman referring to herself as Dinomite69 included a wisecrack comparing her iPhone to using carrier pigeons. At last, I thought, somebody that shares my proclivity for inane topics of conversation. Perhaps I had finally found my soul mate. Sure there were a few problems. For instance, like half of the women on the online dating site I was using, she felt the need to point out on her profile that she had a very unique laugh. In my experience, using such descriptors as unique is often just a cover word for annoying as hell. However, nobody is perfect, so with reckless abandon I made my initial thrust in the swordplay known as finding a mate online.

As a quick aside, it's probably worth mentioning that at this time smartphones were just beginning to become ubiquitous, with around half the adult population owning one. I was not one of these people.

The Message:

I really think you should reconsider carrier pigeon based communication. What a carrier pigeon loses in speed it more then makes up for by being a green technology. Just imagine a world where instead of showing off your new iPhone or Android, you show off your new speckled red crested pigeon, you'll be the envy of all your friends. Plus you get the two side benefits of entering your pigeon in the lucrative Chinese pigeon races (yes, this is a real thing), and putting Pigeon Fancier (one who trains pigeons) on your resume. Really seems like a no brainer to me.

Not to get off the topic of pigeons, but I was wondering what makes your laugh so unique and noticeable? Is it one of those tinkling of heavenly bells laughs, or are we talking about one of those Santa Claus has had way too much eggnog belly laughs? Both are fine, just curious.

The Result:

Dinomite69 probably got too excited about buying carrier pigeons to have time to respond. At least that's what I tell myself. Besides, while carrier pigeons have many advantages over iPhones, they lack reliable internet connection. It was probably impossible for her to get a hold of me after she made the transition.

As a second aside, adding 69 to one's profile name has always been a sure way to let everyone know you are a classy person. I mean, how else would people on a dating site know you are interested in sex? It's even true beyond the world of online dating. I once had a boss who had 69 as part of his business email and people trusted him with millions of dollars.

Attempt #6
LunaGirl

Background:

LunaGirl's profile talked a lot for some reason about how her favorite color was green. I'm not really sure why she felt such a thing was pertinent for a dating profile, but perhaps there was some kind of backstory involving true love only severed by her beloved's irrational hatred of the color. I don't know, or maybe she just didn't want to walk next to someone with a clashing outfit or something. Either way, there really wasn't all that much else in her profile. Under normal conditions I would've probably moved on, but for whatever reason, again not at all related to how attractive she was, I took it as a personal challenge. After all, if there's one thing I don't lack, it's creativity. To help things along, I made up a friend in a little white lie. This is of course not to say that I didn't have friends, just that I didn't have any at the time who had a lot of interest in sitting around talking about the color spectrum.

The Message:

What about teal? I only ask because a friend and I recently got into a debate over whether teal was a shade of green or a shade of blue. Not to put pressure on you, but your profile does suggest you're some kind of green expert, and there may be a substantial bet of $5 riding on the answer.

The Result:

Somehow, beyond reason, this message worked. I guess it always helps to get people talking about what they know. However, much like my earlier success, it didn’t go anywhere. It’s a little hard to branch out into a wider conversation when the only thing you have to build on is a couple of odd comments concerning the color green and a lie.

Attempt #7
Skirtsahoy

Background:

I will say that I'm pretty sure I was slightly drunk or something when I wrote this initial message. It was not the best of times. I was starting to get a bit frustrated with the whole online dating thing. It was a ridiculous amount of work, what with sorting through profiles and trying to decide what the hell to write. Is it any wonder then that eventually one shifted into the zone of being completely bonkers?

The Message:

So, when you say you enjoy scaring the crap out of yourself while watching horror movies, do you mean that figuratively or literally? I'm only asking because I recently got a new Ikea couch (note the subtle hint that I have exquisite taste in furniture) and there is only so many times you can flip a cushion. Plus getting out to Ikea just to buy new cushion covers is a bit of a pain in the ass; what with the drive, the meatballs, etc. Now there are always exceptions, but in general I'd say I consider defecating on my furniture a deal breaker.

However, I really have no problem with you peeing and throwing up on yourself while riding a roller coaster. I'm fairly classy and wouldn't even do the whole pretend I don't know you thing. Nope, I'd walk proud with you through the amusement park for the rest of the day. Though I'd probably leave my window down on the car ride home.

The Result:

For the safety of my furniture and car seats it was probably better that someone who stated that they liked to scare the crap out of themselves while watching scary movies and pee themselves on roller coasters did not respond back. I’m not really sure what I would’ve done if she had.

Attempt #8
BailaSalsa

Background:

You get to see all types while perusing online dating profiles, and one must always be ready to use whatever opening they can to try and get their message to pop up above the crowd. However, one must always remember that it's a fine line between playfully poking fun at someone and actively making fun of them. BailaSalsa's profile gave the impression that she had a fascination with the movie *Clue*, which is fair, given that *Clue* is awesome, what with its multiple endings and all. However, it also mentioned that her high school class had voted her most likely to go skydiving. She was twenty-seven. This was perhaps the first attempt I made where I really didn't put all that much work into it.

The Message:

Sure you were voted most likely to go sky diving, but did you actually do it?

I'm fully with you on Clue being a great movie, one of the more under appreciated ones in my opinion. Which was your favorite ending?

The Result:

Now I admittedly don't know much about the best way to flirt with the fairer sex, but I do know that pointing out someone's flaws is probably not the best way to get them to talk to you. But then again, if they're bragging about being voted most likely to go skydiving in high school, and then never do it, they probably don't have good follow through anyways.

Attempt #9
Cakesfen

Background:

Cakesfen's profile seemed to suggest that she really enjoyed running and drinking, so of course I had to introduce her to the Hash House Harriers, the infamous drinking club with a running problem. Basically, a bunch of people get together, drink beer, go on some type of amalgamation of a run and scavenger hunt, and then sing ribald songs. Being a hasher myself, it was a perfect opening, or at least it would've been if I hadn't gone on from there deep into crazy town.

The Message:

Sometimes when I'm using this thing I get an uncomfortable sensation that OkCupid is far too similar to buying a car stereo off of Amazon. Really all its missing is just a section for comments from other people who have tried the "product". These are the times that I wonder how somebody talked me into trying this thing.

Lets face some facts. Your an attractive woman who seems to have an interesting personality, so I imagine you get a large number of messages from random guys, of which a creepily large amount contain pictures of abs. Given this sheer volume little old me doesn't stand much of a chance of being noticed, especially since I am not gifted with the ability to start a conversation via email. I propose that, if you're in anyway interested, we cut all this crap and just get a happy hour drink sometime. At worst you lose just an hour of one day of your life.

Irregardless your above desicion. After perusing your profile I picked up a few hints that you like to run, explore Portland, and inbibe in alcoholic beverages. I guess I'm a regular Sherlock Holmes. I belong to a drinking/running group called the Hash House Harriers and I think it might be something you'd be interested in. We meet up several times a week to have a few beers, go on a run, and generally just have a good time. The two big selling points are each time it starts in a different point in the city, and only one person knows where the run is going to go.

Shawn

P.S. Kudos on looking good enough in a lavender bridesmaid dress that the dude on the motorcycle stopped to check you out.

The Result:

In retrospect, women rarely like getting compared to car stereos, even highly rated ones. They say honesty is the best policy, but when it comes to online dating, that's kind of a load of bullshit. Slightly related, I'm not sure why I felt the need to include my actual name at the end.

Attempt #10
Sek8219

Background:

Sek8219's profile seemed very concerned over the possibility of a zombie apocalypse. Knowing that women like a man that makes them feel safe, I wanted to convey that I was a man of action with a plan for just such an eventuality.

The Message:

I believe that everyone needs to have a zombie apocalypse escape plan. If year's of watching public service announcements has taught me anything, its be prepared.

My zombie escape plans involves an armored bus carrying at least 15 survivors with very mismatched personalities to the area of the state with the lowest population density. I envision it to be similar to MTV's Road Rules, only with zombies. I estimate that in our journey at least 5 people will die, 3 being minor characters, 1 being a major douchebag who hides the fact that he's been infected, and 1 being the most skilled character who has shown the most heroism and wisdom during the journey.

When we build our new utopian city, we will name it after him/her.

The Result:

Believe it or not, but for whatever reason this message worked. Probably because I was humble enough not to name the new utopian city after myself. Messages back and forth eventually led to a date, the first one I had managed to get in this mad adventure, but alas, it was not to be. Where communication via the written word had flowed like water, the spoken variety was but a trickle between us.

As a quick note, if spelling and grammar mistakes drive you nuts, oh boy is a lot of this book going to be a tough read for you.

Attempt #11
EmRocker

Background:

Buoyed by something at least a little bit close to success, I threw myself back into the online dating world, confident that it would only be a matter of time. The next profile to catch my eye was that of EmRocker. It was a strange one, containing quite a few comments regarding slug sex. While this was obviously red flag central, my boost in confidence led me to decide that there was no risk too great. Besides, thanks to recently watching a slugcentric episode of Isabella Rosellini's *Green Porn*, a YouTube show that described how various animals mate, I had a vast knowledge of gastropod coital rituals. It almost seemed like fate. Though in retrospect given it was a fairly popular video series on YouTube at the time, it might have been more just similar YouTube algorithm results, but in today's electronic world, that's pretty much fate too, I guess.

The Message:

Who isn't amazed by hot slug on slug action? Though to be honest, I have been a little traumatized since I learned that sometimes they chew each others penises off. However, regardless of my personal feelings I remember recently seeing a video on the subject and laughing my ass off. Enjoy.

Shawn

The Result:

EmRocker must have already known all my slug sex fun facts and decided I had nothing new to offer because I never heard even a peep out of her.

This was also the second instance of me ending the message with my actual name. I'm not really sure why I was doing this, but perhaps I wanted to make myself seem more trustworthy or something, or perhaps I was just tired of feeling more like a profile than an actual person. Hard to say. Regardless, it became a bit of habit moving forward.

Attempt #12
Varleigh

Background:

Varleigh's profile was one of the more enjoyable out of all the ones I had perused so far. It was a straightforward profile, succinctly not only stating who she was, but also what she wanted. It gave the impression that she had a good head on her shoulders and a realistic expectation of what a relationship entails. To add icing to the cake, her pictures gave clues that she was the kind of woman who knew how to have fun. They included one of her wearing deer antlers, one of her holding a machete, and one of her holding a stack of empty beer cans taped together, a configuration better known as a wizard's staff. How could I not message her?

The Message:

Refering to what your wrote for the most private thing you're willing to admit, rock on. After reading it, and looking over the rest of your profile, a voice in my head said to me, "this woman obviously has her shit together, you should message her."
"But what the hell would I say?" I asked.

"You'll figure something out," answered the voice, "just be honest and straightforward. Also probably avoid making the obvious nice rack joke."

"C'mon, it would be hilarious." I said.

"No," said the voice forcefully, "if you want to say something about her pics complement that sweet ass machete she has, or ask her how tall she managed to get that wizard staff."

"That is a pretty rad machete."

"Indeed."

Anyway, that was the inner monologue that led to me sending this message. Maybe its a little too much for a first time message but I hope you at least get a laugh out of it. Though I would still like to know how tall that wizard staff got?

Shawn

The Result:

Did it work? Damn straight it worked. I got a message back and before I knew it we had managed to have a nice long conversation centering on how tall each of us had managed to get our respective wizard staffs. Unfortunately, like all stars that shine too bright, things burned out soon after. The messages began having much longer delays between them, and eventually I had to accept that things had fizzled. Such are the risks of online dating.

Attempt #13
TwoNightLights

Background:

Smarting from my latest defeat, I was glad to soon after find a profile that entertained me greatly. TwoNightLights bragged about being able to give good airplane rides, wherein one person lays on their back with their legs in the air while a second holds themselves out horizontally while balanced on the first person's feet. She also had a crazy made-up story that she was going to be competing in a llama wrestling match, which apparently, at least according to her description, is more of a staring contest rather than an actual grapple. Either way, it was the right combination of well thought out absurdity to catch my interest.

The Message:

I started writing this only hoping to score some sweet airplane rides, but then I read the rest of your profile.

Good luck to you in your upcoming Llama Wrestling competition with the unfazeable Mr. Professor. He's a dangerous opponent, and probably one of the greatest llamas to ever participate in the sport. I remember watching him during the '07 World Championship in Helsinki. He and Felipe Rostov, the reigning champ at the time, battled for over 14 hours. Finally Mr. Rostov fell over dead from a brain aneurism. For god sakes, be careful.

Shawn

P.S. Also congrats on your fine work bringing back the word heiney.

The Result:

I got no response. Perhaps llama wrestling is a real thing, but then again, maybe she was just a crazy person, in which case I'm probably better off that she never responded.

Attempt #14
BrighterQuicker

Background:

This prospective mate talked about the Urban Iditarod in her profile, a formerly annual event in Portland where teams in coordinated costumes pulled shopping carts across the city from bar to bar. As you can imagine, it was a bit of a drunken mess, which is probably why it doesn't happen anymore. Having been a regular participant myself, it really seemed like a no brainer. I kept it simple and did my best to hide the fact that I'm weird.

The Message:

Realistically what kind of people haven't heard of Urban Iditarod? I've done it twice so far, once as part of the Venture Brothers team and last year as part of the probably entirely inappropriate Whitney Houston pallbearers team. What about you?

Shawn

The Result:

BrighterQuicker replied! All hail the power of the Urban Iditarod, may it rest in peace. Not only did she reply, but the messages soon after led to me getting my second actual date since starting my online dating campaign. The date itself seemed to go well, with her even saying she'd be glad to have a second, but unfortunately, by the time I tried to schedule the said second date, she had apparently changed her mind. Such is life.

Just so you know, when I say inappropriate Whitney Houston pallbearers' team, I mean really damn inappropriate. She had just died a week earlier, and we constantly snorted lines of flour off of the cardboard casket we had made to the point that I was blowing dough out of my nose for a week or two afterwards. I was young and dumb, a common occurrence when one is overly full of the precious resource we call life.

Attempt #15
PDXGal8

Background:

I was starting to get fed up with the whole online dating thing. Sure, I had managed to get two dates, but overall it didn't seem to be worth all the work I was putting into it. Perhaps that's why things began to spiral into a strange desperation. The strategy of keeping things focused fell apart, replaced by a shotgun of openers in hopes that one would hit home. PDXGal8's profile stated that she liked poetry, wanted to go on a treasure hunt, and enjoyed talking about sociology. I went in with all guns blazing.

The Message:

How do I stand out,
Just one more face in the crowd,
But so very much more.

I do not have a treasure map...yet. But I have been working on piecing together clues from old Oregon Trail journals to try and find the lost Blue Bucket Mine. This is just one of the many brands I have in the fire.

I also enjoy a talking about societal structures and theorizing on why things are the way they are. Unfortunately its often hard to find people who want to talk about such things, especially if the two of you disagree. This seems funny to me since listening to dissenting opinions is often the best way learn.

Shawn

The Result:

Apparently, my haiku sucked because I never got a response. The bit about looking for the lost Blue Bucket Mine is true, which I never found, or at least that's what I tell people.

Now at this point some people might find my frustration regarding rejection by fewer women than I had fingers and toes a bit strange, especially those use to the swiping app model which dominates online dating today. However, to give a little context, at the time I had only ever dated in the real world, which had the benefit of giving me the opportunity to scope out the general vibe and signs of them being attracted to me before approaching them. Online dating was a new thing, and none of us had really gotten use to the countless number of rejections which we now consider normal.

Attempt #16
Mountain-Seeker

Background:

Things continued to degrade with each failure, though this was not how I viewed it in my mind at the time. Mountain-Seeker's profile included a lot of song lyrics, including part of a song by The Doors, so of course I thought it was clever to put in the next few lines from the song. The fact that I had to look up the lyrics online should've been a clue that this wasn't the best of ideas. To be fair, it wasn't like her profile gave me a whole lot to work with. The only other thing of interest was that she knew how to make lemonade by letting lemons mold in water.

The Message:

I see you live on Love Street
There's this store where the creatures meet
I wonder what they do in there

Lyrics from The Doors and promises to clean my fridge to make moldy lemonade. How could I resist?

My day has been a little strange. It started out normal enough with showering, shaving, eating breakfast. But then I left my wallet in the refrigerator and it has all just kind of gone downhill from there. Now here I am, wasting time, perusing the internet.

Anyways, I should probably get back to work. Message me back if you want to.

Shawn

The Result:

In a word, nope. However, on the lighter side I didn't have to try lemonade made out of moldy lemons or deal with somebody who quotes song lyrics to describe themselves. So you know, silver linings.

Attempt #17
PDXrach

Background:

My first experience of online dating had worn me down to a nub. With so many possibilities it was easy to find reasons to avoid messaging people, making it mean just that much more when an acceptable prospective mate presented themselves. Every initial message was a piece of myself. A sacrifice of time and effort to the possibility of future coupled happiness, most of which popped as easy as a soap bubble, destroying in an instant the potential world which I had created in my mind.

All together PDXrach had a pretty good profile. It was a smattering of random thoughts and factoids, a combination I would have earlier judged, but had come to accept as a mirror of my own scattered psyche. There were several parts that stuck out. In addition to a series of questions she claimed plagued her every day, she also included a joke based on the game of *Clue*, claiming she had killed a man with a pipe in the conservatory. She also bragged about her *MarioKart* abilities and had a picture of her brandishing a Christmas tree like a weapon.

The Message:

Damn it, I was guessing in the billiard room with the wrench, boy was I off.

Anyways, though I am no expert and I'm absolutely not licensed in any way by any credible institution or organization, I believe I can provide suitable answers for all of the things you spend a lot of time thinking about.

You should eat food for dinner. In order to stay healthy you should avoid eating plastic fish, they are not food and present a choking hazard. The best way to get around town without a car is to learn how to fly. Learning how to fly is easy, you just throw yourself at the ground and miss. The best way to get out of town without a car is to hitchhike with truckers, they always have interesting stories and only 1 in 10 will probably murder you. For second dinner you should probably stick with food, though moss is a suitable substitute if you want to mix it up a bit. Luckily Portland has no shortage of moss, and its all organic. Thinking about your loved ones is good, though if you really cared you'd probably offer them some of your primo locally grown organic moss.

I hope this helps.

Shawn

P.S. Not to brag, but I could probably kick your ass in Mario Kart, except for Rainbow Road, that level is seriously screwed up. However, you probably have me beat in the ancient art of beating the crap out of people with Christmas trees.

The Result:

Despite my best attempts, it worked. I even got a pretty witty response back. Unfortunately, that's where things ended. The second message was not as lucky as the first. In retrospect, it might have been for the best. Perhaps her comment regarding killing a man actually had nothing to do with *Clue*. Such is the danger of making assumptions.

The First Hiatus

With the failure of my seventeenth attempt, I was completely drained. Sure, I had managed to get some responses and a couple of dates, but overall, the experience was exhausting and decidedly strange. Not wishing to suffer the constant pain of rejection, at least for a little while, I decided to take a hiatus from the online dating world. My profile sat abandoned, silent in the void.

To those used to the rapid swiping of today's online dating apps, it might seem strange for me to quit after only seventeen attempts. But this was a different time and a different place. As previously stated, profiles were longer and there was a greater expectation that people would actually read them and that messages would be tailored to the individual. Just deciding on whether to message somebody was an endeavor unto itself, with countless profiles gone through before a message was even considered. Even worse, this was before matching, so one could go through all of this painstaking and time-consuming process, only to send a message to someone who had absolutely no interest in you whatsoever. It was a grind, and in that way, much more similar to actually meeting strangers in the real world compared to the present iteration.

That's not to say that some people didn't take a more mass marketing approach to things. Early pioneers were already just sending a simple message of some version of hello to as many women as possible. I had a friend who told me it was the best way to go given she had met that last several people she had dated in such a manner. However, given none of these relationships lasted more than a few weeks, I had a hard time agreeing with her point of view. Perhaps I was just naïve, but it didn't feel like the best way to connect with someone beyond the 'yeah, I'd probably fuck them' level.

In the end it was only a matter of time. One could call it quits, but the siren song was bound to draw me in again. The reasons I had started online dating persisted. They say there are many fish in the sea, but there is no fishing hole quite so filled to the brim as online dating. Sure, I had never caught anything in those teeming waters, but I knew people who had and if they could do it, why couldn't I do it too? I just needed to be a little more patient and perhaps just a bit more charming. In the end, loneliness and lust overcame all doubts. So it was that after several months in the real world, I returned to the electronic meat market, ready to further refine my skills in creating the ever-elusive perfect initial message.

Attempt #18
RockStarGoddess

Background:

After combing through numerous profiles to find the perfect woman to mark the restarting of my quest, I soon grew overwhelmed and settled on just selecting someone attractive, though not so attractive that I thought them out of my league. RockStarGoddess' profile was all over the place, so I strategically decided to shotgun a whole bunch of comments at her at once to see if any would stick. She mentioned in her profile that she only wanted "real" people to contact her, which I felt fit me pretty well. She also had some strange comments regarding Bohemian fabric and the movie *Melancholia*.

The Message:

This might seem a silly question, but I don't have any idea what would be considered Bohemian fabric? For some reason I picture it having to do with the philosopical Bohemians, not the Czech ones.

Also, please rest assured that I am real. I did go through a short phase of wondering if I was just a figment of my cat's imagination, but the cat died and I'm still here, so that theory was shot pretty full of holes.

Shawn

P.S. Relax, I have it on good authority that Melancholia is going to miss the Earth. Though I have noticed a lot of symbolic slow motion sequences taking place recently.

The Result:

I never got to find out what the hell is Bohemian fabric. I guess I could look it up, but what's the fun in that? Anyways, RockStarGoddess didn't send back any kind of response, which unfortunately for me, kicked off a serious existential crisis where I wondered if I was truly just a figment of my dead cat's imagination.

Attempt #19
Olivialive

Background:

They say that one of the best ways to get someone's attention is to create a bridge of commonality, show them that the two of you share similar values and experiences, thus giving you something to talk about. However, sometimes a profile has little to nothing in it, which in turn forces one to look for things in common that in the grand scheme of things don't really mean shit. A good example of this would be this attempt, a woman who had little to offer about herself other than the fact that she was taller than average and tired of people mentioning it all the time. Being a tall man myself, it seemed a perfect fit.

The Message:

I as well have never been able to figure out why people feel the need to mention how tall I am. It's not like I never noticed before. Their next question always inevitably seems to be whether or not I play basketball. Its too bad that tallism is so rampant in our society. Maybe we need to have a parade or something?

My brother, who is even taller, once had a random lady in the grocery store ask him how tall he was. He returned with asking how much she weighed. She got mad and told him that some things are just rude to ask. He said, "exactly." Unfortunately his point seemed to go right over her head.

Crap now I'm making tall jokes. I'm going to wrap this up before the poor puns get out of hand.

Shawn

The Result:

Few things bring people together quite like suffering from the same prejudice. Olivialive replied and over time our mutual hatred of people who feel the need to point out the obvious grew our bond until we both felt comfortable actually meeting in person. Unfortunately, that's when things took a turn for the worst. As it turns out, you can't really build a relationship just off of both being taller than average.

Attempt #20
Sophiebpbp

Background:

The success of actually getting a date after just two initial messages following my hiatus probably went to my head more than it should have. Maybe that's why I felt cocky enough to fully let my freak flag fly. Sophiebpbp's profile claimed she had the best job in the universe. I don't remember exactly what it was, maybe a teacher or jazzercise instructor or something, but my boundless imagination really doubted it was true. I might have completely skipped over her profile, which also mentioned that she enjoyed card games, if it hadn't been for what appeared to be a good sense of humor. She joked that she liked watching street fights, so I thought, what the hell, might as well not hold back.

The Message:

I'm afraid I must disagree with you. The best job in the universe is being the personal lion tamer for Teddy Roosevelt. But since Teddy is long dead I will concede that your job may possibly be the best job in the universe currently.

I personally find street fights to be a little old hat. These days I'm into more current crazes like underground Kangaroo boxing.

Shawn

P.S. I'll take you in cards any day of the week, except Bridge. Despite the newspaper printing Bridge tips every week, I have no interest in playing.

The Result:

I didn't hear anything back from her, though this was probably only because of a severe bout of depression brought on by her realizing that her job actually wasn't the best one in the universe. Either that or perhaps the only card game she liked was Bridge.

Attempt #21
Urbanbambi

Background:

Time to be a little honest about things. I'm attracted to crazy. I know it's not healthy and that at times it can even be dangerous, but for whatever reason nothing gets my motor running quite like someone slightly off their rocker. That's probably why I decided that it would be a good idea to send a message to a woman whose profile made a point of bragging that she still had all of her fingers and toes, and then went on to demand that any man who messaged her had to be able to carry her with little to no effort if her legs fell off due to leprosy. However, the cherry on top of the crazy sundae had to be the fact that she included a link on her profile to her brother's profile. I'm not sure what the point of it was. It's not like I'd be looking at her profile and suddenly just change my mind and decide that I wanted to date dudes.

The Message:

Congratulations on having all of your fingers and toes. I was going to write more but then got strangely caught up in reading your brother's profile to see if he was as hilarious as you described. Now I'm a little rushed so I can get to bed at a decent hour.

Shawn

P.S. I am willing to carry your legless leprous body for a mile if your legs made up a significant portion of your body weight and you agree that if we ever get involved at a chicken fight at the pool, I get to be on top.

The Result:

There's nothing crazy likes quite like crazy. While she sent a message back, it was mostly to quiz me on her brother's profile to prove that I actually hadn't read it. Questions I easily answered given that I only claim to do things if I've actually done them. Our messages back and forth then broke down into negotiations which ended with me giving up being the top rung in a chicken fight for the guarantee of always getting to be the wheelbarrow in any unplanned wheelbarrow races. Unfortunately, it was all for naught, for she soon after broke off communication.

Attempt #22
CAP84

Background:

Anytime a woman say she loves herself some Jack Handy, the delightful advice giver from old Saturday Night Live episodes, you know I'm going to try and make a move. That's just good old fashioned common sense. That being said, I felt it was important to try and clarify exactly what kind of person she was looking for given that her profile explicitly stated that certain types of people should not try to contact her.

The Message:

My favorite Jack Handy is as follows (please excuse the paraphrasing):

"When you're a child walking to school there is nothing worse then getting splashed by a passing car hitting a puddle. You stand there, wondering if you should go to school sodden and wet, or go home to change and be late for school. So while the kid was sitting there wondering, I drove by and splashed him again."

……

And crap, I've just wasted a half hour reading Jack Handey quotes, many of which are better then the one I thought was my favorite.

Shawn

P.S. I once did play dead at a business meeting, unfortunately nobody noticed.

P.P.S Is it all right to message you if your both good company and a bathroom stall type of good time?

The Result:

Mysteriously I never heard back from her. I'm guessing CAP84 was just saying that she was a Jack Handy fan in a lame attempt to sound cool. Pretty pathetic on her part if you ask me. As a side note, I have absolutely no memory what the hell the whole thing with playing dead in a business meeting was about.

Attempt #23
LittleLimaBee

Background:

A woman who claims that she might accidentally start the Norse apocalypse. Of course I'm going to message her. Someone who thinks people who drive hybrid cars are assholes. Even better. A member of the fairer sex who loves the novels of Douglas Adams. Christmas has come early. Now how in the hell do I impress her?

The Message:

So, your friends say that you are the most likely person to start an apocalypse, and then you take a "Mythological Profile" test and get Jormungand. Your friends might be onto something there.

I was reading a study the other day, and by that I mean reading an article on a humor website that cited a study, that had some statistical data showing that people who drive hybrid cars are less courteous compared to the average driver. The theory is that since they see themselves doing a good deed, it becomes easier for them to justify being less courteous (i.e. I'm saving the world, so forgetting to use my blinker is really no big deal). Maybe it works the same way for bikers.

Shawn

P.S. Forty-two is the exact number of minutes that the average diner will wait before they go from, "when you have a second," to, "holy shit where the hell is my food." It is unknown if this is related to the mathematics involved in splitting a restaurant check.

The Result:

Believe it or not the above words pulled straight out of my ass somehow worked. Apparently, women just can’t resist a knowledgeable man willing to talk about the end of the world and why people are sometimes jackasses. Unfortunately, that’s as far as it got. After a couple of messages back and forth things petered out. Back to the drawing board.

Attempt #24
Hello_Panda

Background:

In her profile, Hello_Panda mentioned that she enjoyed sniffing laundry detergent. Now most people would find that a little weird, but I've just kind of learned to roll with things since I'm a little weird myself.

The Message:

Sniffing the laundry detergent makes a lot of sense. Nobody wants all of their clothes to smell like something unpleasant. I'm going to start doing it. If anybody asks me why I'm sniffing all of the detergent's in the store, I'll just go all crazy eyed and tell them its to get high.

Please don't take this to be rude, I don't know and I'm just curious, but what does a Geography major write a thesis about?

Shawn

P.S. I also like sharing dishes at restaurants so I can try more things. Though I've learned its better to ask people before I do it.

The Result:

She didn't answer, but I imagine she was having a pretty rough time when she realized that nobody in their right mind would ever read a Geography thesis. Either that or she was too busy trying to get high on laundry detergent.

In a tangentially related aside, when I was in college, I lived next to a laundromat, so my buddy would come over and drink beer and watch movies while he waited for his laundry to be done. One time we went down to get his clothes out of the dryer and we discovered a woman opening his drier. Not yet being noticed, and assuming she was just taking his clothes out in order to use the dryer, we hung back to see how things played out. Still not noticing us, or at least I assume, she took out a pair of his freshly laundered tighty-whiteys and gave them a deep audible sniff and then sighed deeply with pleasure. We snuck out and came back later. Now I'm pretty sure that Hello_Panda wasn't the same person but wouldn't that have been a strange coincidence.

Attempt #25
LsOm

Background:

It was at this point that things began to go downhill. One failure after another cut down my faith in the idea that I would ever meet somebody. Depression began to set in, which of course led to drinking, which as one can easily imagine, led to overly philosophical messages.

I don't really remember anything about LsOM's profile, other than apparently she was a big lover of wine and good friends, which doesn't really seem like all that interesting of a factoid.

The Message:

Like many things in life I think wine and friends are on a sliding scale. The higher the quality of the drinking partners, the more I'm willing to put up with poor quality wine. Conversely, the higher the quality of the wine, the more I'm willing to put up with poor quality company. To have both good wine and good friends in one sitting, now that's just a good thing.

The Result:

LsOm must have assumed that I had access to really high-quality wine. I never heard a peep out of her.

Attempt #26
SparklingLava

Background:

Perhaps it was the drink that convinced me it would be a good idea to message a woman who stated in her profile that what she was really looking for was an open relationship with Amy Poehler and Will Arnett. I hated having to be the one to break the bad news to her, but on the plus side, it gave me a pretty solid opening. SparklingLava's profile also stated that she hated hipsters because they always felt the need to show off how they knew the names of more obscure bands than her.

The Message:

I'm sorry to have to be the one to tell you, but Amy Poehler and Will Arnett are breaking up. You could probably still get involved in an open relationship with them, but it would probably be fairly awkward. I imagine a lot of snide comments, though the sex would probably be pretty good.

Wow, when I go back and read the last paragraph that's a terrible way to start a conversation. But in all honesty these kind of things run through my head quite a bit, so I'm just going to leave it.

Also, if you get involved in a who's heard of more bands conversation, couldn't you just start making up band names, I mean, who's really going to know.

The Result:

I never got a reply, but I wasn't all that surprised. Who has time to message some online dolt when you're busy buying tickets to Hollywood so you can hook up with Amy and/or Will? I can't really blame her. We all have to follow our dreams. Also, initial messages are probably not the best time for introspection.

Attempt #27
Blueflame9732

Background:

I tried to take this one at least a little seriously given that Bluflame9732's profile made her seem like a pretty nice woman. She was originally from Vermont and liked to play scrabble. She seemed like the kind of genuine person you'd have no second thoughts about taking to meet your parents.

The Message:

I know that its probably blasphemous to a person from Vermont, but for some reason I've always preferred the fake maple syrup. I don't know why. I've tried countless different real maple syrups, driven by the idea that I should like the real more then the fake, but its no good. Maybe its because that's what we always had when I was a kid. King corn got me young.

On a different note, I'm probably not better at scrabble. I'm not saying that I have a poor vocabulary. But I seem to have a bad habit of drawing mostly vowels whenever I play. My strategy largely consists of waiting until someone puts down a really high scoring word, and then putting a "S" on the end.

The Result:

I got a reply, but it was mostly just to call me a blasphemer for not using real maple syrup. I was a little disappointed. It's not every day I just give away my winning scrabble strategies.

Attempt #28
Seren_K

Background:

My introspective state just seemed to get worse with every message. While one should never lie when writing initial messages, filtering yourself somewhat is probably not a bad idea. Before letting people know that you're just a little nuts, you need to give them a chance to get to know your better qualities that make putting up with the rest worthwhile. Unfortunately, I didn't do any of that and my messages just kind of collapsed into spouting out the first thing that came to mind. Seren_K's profile claimed that she had a really thick Minnesota accent that she was trying to hide. She also stated that two big factors she was looking for in a prospective mate were that they didn't care about getting yellow lab hair on black pants and that they had their shit together.

The Message:

If I was you I'd quit trying to shake the Minnesota accent and instead just ham it up to an extreme that can only be described as awkward for everyone around you.

Anyways, I should probably not just write the first thing that pops into my head on these things, but it seems like the most honest thing to do. The whole thing with the yellow lab hair on black pants seems pretty specific. Have you had trouble with that before?

Also, please rest assured that I have my shit together. I eat a lot of fiber so this has never been a problem. This seems like something really personal to wonder about people though.

The Result:

No reply, though I wasn't really all that disappointed. The Minnesota accent has to be one of the least sexy of accents, at least in my opinion, for dirty talk. That being said, if someone would like to prove me wrong, I'm game to give it a go.

Attempt #29
Hufflepie

Background:

The next profile that caught my eye included a triple exposure picture where it looked like three of Hufflepie were sitting at a restaurant booth having a conversation. I thought it was a pretty creative profile picture, so of course I wanted to let her know my appreciation via my own creativity.

The Message:

You on the left in your third picture down does not seem very interested in what you on the right is saying. She just has that look like she wishes she was anywhere else. At least middle you is pretending to pay attention, even though she's actually just wondering if its too early to order a third beer and why you on the right is being so serious.

The Result:

I never heard back from her. Maybe I was mistaken and Hufflepie was really one of a set of triplets.

Attempt #30
Red_Gemini

Background:

As my frustration with the whole online dating process grew, my messages began to get shorter and shorter. I was getting tired of putting in a huge amount of effort with little to no reward. The quality of things that attracted me also seemed to decline at an alarming rate. For instance, what caught my eye in this woman's profile was the claim that she was good at pretending to be Kristen Wiig and putting her foot in her mouth.

The Message:

So wait.....are the pretending to be Kristin Wigg and putting your foot in your mouth dependent on each other, or independent of each other. If their dependent on each other you might have the makings of a great stage act.

The Result:

Was I successful? Nope. However, I still think her combined talents would've made for one hell of a great stage act.

Attempt #31 Squarerootofneg1

Background:

After several short messages I managed to perk myself up enough to put some effort back into it. Unfortunately, perusing through the various profiles, I probably let the pendulum swing back too far the other way. Squarerootofneg1 seemed nice. Maybe too nice. Her comments mostly were based around the book she was reading and the fact that she disliked texting. It kind of seemed like the profile your mother middle-aged mother would put up.

The Message:

Congratulations on avoiding the use of emoticons. I've always found them annoying and have avoided using them as much as possible. I don't really like texting either, though the ever moving tide of societal norms has forced me to accept it as a general part of my day to day life. Granted, a large part of my anti-text stance is probably due to my stubborn refusal to upgrade from my current flip phone.

I'm a one book at a time kind of person myself, but I can understand the allure of being able to switch them out. Sorry to hear the non-fiction is always getting neglected. I feel like there's a lot of poorly written non-fiction out there, which is too bad, because a lot of the stories are really interesting. I just got done with a non-fiction about a cult called the Holy Rollers that was in Corvallis back in 1905. It was really well written and kept me pretty captivated.

The Result:

Did I get a reply? Hell yeah I got a reply. The drought was finally over, at least for a little while. We messaged back and forth for a bit, but it didn't really go anywhere, probably because in many ways Squarerootofneg1 was just boring as shit, or not crazy if you prefer, which really puts more of the onus on me. On another note, you should really learn more about that sex cult in Corvallis, Oregon back in 1905. That shit was nuts.

Attempt #32
Ktt_486

Background:

I was getting close to giving up on the whole online dating thing, but before I did, I decided to throw up a Hail Mary pass of bluntness. A declaration to the world, or at least to one poor woman in it, that here I am, crazy and all.

The Message:

Hello fellow tall person. I will openly admit that I'm becoming kind of bored with this OkCupid thing and I'm pretty much now just writing messages to entertain myself in some kind of weird experiment to see whether or not people will respond. Strangely enough my response rate has not really decreased any, but the dates I have gone on have gotten more entertaining.

You claim to be a creative swearer, a quality I take great pride in myself exhibiting, lets hear what you got.

Also I noticed that the six things you could never do without rearranged a little bit make a nice little story about two people hooking up. Friends, hugs, exercise, orgasms, purpose, good sleep.

The Result:

Believe it or not, but this actually worked. I got a reply, but soon after Ktt_486 closed her account. So yeah, that was a first. Also, creative swearer my ass.

Attempt #33 Waderlustforlyf

Background:

It was the end of the line for me. I couldn't do it anymore. The whole experience of online dating was too draining to keep it up. However, like any great athlete, I decided to give it my all in one last desperate attempt. The last lucky woman's profile said that she wanted to hang out with a mostly nice person who would get a little tipsy and converse with her. There was no doubt in my mind that I could easily meet such qualifications.

The Message:

I am mostly a nice person who enjoys getting moderately tipsy with strangers. As evidence that I'm a nice guy I have never had a picture taken showing off my abs or standing next to a really cool car. As for the part about getting tipsy, you'll just have to take my word on it.

Talking with total strangers can sometimes be weird because you never know what subjects are going to interest them, so for the sake of efficiency here are some subjects I could cover over a few beers:

1) What your original hair color was. I'm a good guesser.
2) What is the answer to 6 down.
3) Points in life that make you feel relatively old.
4) What the people on the date across the room are probably saying.
5) The current socio-economic issues in China.
6) Tales from my abnormal childhood on a large cattle ranch in the middle of nowhere.
7) The sorta creepy fact that OkCupid is kind of like shopping on Amazon.
8) What the hell is going to happen on Game of Thrones.
9) What happens when we die?
10) A multitude of random fun facts.

The Result:

With the last of my strength, I strived for the goal, and fell far short. I never heard anything back from Wanderlustforlyf. Perhaps I should have included some abs pictures.

The Second Hiatus

It was the end of the line. I couldn't do it anymore. I accepted that perhaps I was destined to be alone, or if not, my partner in crime wasn't to be found on the worldwide web. I shut off my profile again, though as with the last time I did not delete it. I don't know what stopped me, perhaps just the belief that one never knows what the future might hold.

This was the state of things for nine months, which might seem like a long time to quit anything, especially if that thing may help fill what some call a basic need. Oh yes, I had a lot of trepidation about re-entering the world of online dating, but as they say, you never get anywhere if you don't try.

With this in mind, I not only reactivated my profile, but also completely revamped it to better represent the totally different person I now was thanks to nine months of personal reflection and, if we are being honest about it, probably a little too much heavy drinking. Plunging in headfirst, I started perusing the world of possible mates, hoping beyond hope that maybe this time I'd come up with an initial message so amazing that it would catch somebody's eye and make them swoon. It would have to be creative.

Attempt #34
HikingGirl29

Background:

The first girl I dared to message after revamping my profile mentioned on hers that she still used a flip phone. This instantly threw up a green flag for me since I as well was refusing to move on to a better form of communication technology. Risking the fact that she might be a hipster, I sent her a message.

The Message:

Kudos to you for avoiding upgrading your flip phone. I am a fellow flip phone user (flip phoner, flip phonest, flip phonista?) who despite years of ridicule has also refused to upgrade. The flip phone has tons of advantages over newer phones, including:

1) I never have to worry if I'm making a phone call or taking a picture.
2) I still get lost sometimes, allowing for new random discoveries.
3) I get to pretend I'm Captain Kirk every time I make a call.

4) If I purposefully miss a call I can blame it on my shitty old phone.
5) Conversations are better since I can't just look up the answer.

Stand strong.

Shawn

P.S. When I looked at your bottom picture the Indiana Jones theme song started playing in my head.

The Result:

I think I probably talked her out of keeping her flip phone. I imagine she was too busy going to the mall to buy a smartphone to message me back.

On a slightly tangential topic, though not quite ubiquitous, by this time smartphones were definitely well on their way to becoming the integral part of our culture that they are today, with only a few holdouts like myself remaining, especially amongst the younger age brackets. While I'm not sure why I resisted for as long as I did, I went to some interesting lengths to avoid giving in. For example, when I got lost, I'd use what I called Jeff Maps, which was me calling my friend Jeff, who had a smartphone, and describing where I was and where I was trying to go so he could look up directions for me. This went on for a surprisingly long amount of time. Jeff is overall a pretty patient guy.

Attempt #35
Vonnegoodtomeetya

Background:

For some reason when I first started online dating again it seemed necessary to try and hide how weird I am. I tried sending nice normal messages (though reading back through them it became obvious that this plan was an utter failure). I don't know what I was thinking, maybe the plan was to wait until they had a lot of time invested with me, so they were less likely to run when they figured out I'm a weirdo.

The Message:

I've never read any Vonnegut before, though I imagine he should be on the list. I hope this isn't held against me. I have read quite a bit of Heller, who at the very least was one of Vonnegut's good literary friends, so maybe that's worth something.

I recently watched the League and it inspired me to let some of my friends talk me into joining their fantasy football league. I have been disappointed, though in fairness my expectations for zany adventures were probably unrealistic.

I recently got back from Panama (for fun) and I'm going to go to Japan and China in December (for work). But the next place I really want to go is Skellig Michael.

Well, those are some things about me. If you want to message me back I'd be interested in learning some more things about you.

Shawn

The Result:

I got a message. We went back and forth a bit and went out on a date which didn't lead anywhere. I guess liking two different authors who were friends back when they were still alive is probably not the best recipe for success.

On a side note, I cannot state how much my foray into fantasy football was a complete and utter waste of my time. At the very least I expected some amazing shit talking, but in the end it was just a bunch of people who want an excuse to pay attention to absolutely every football game. I guess that's what I get for basing my expectations on a TV show.

Attempt #36
JulieFoodie

Background:

I continued on my quest of trying to fake being a normal person. This made it really hard to write initial messages since most people pretty much put the exact same things in their profiles. The number of women with pictures of rock climbing or somewhere exotic was insane. The only thing I could pick out of this one was that she liked the movie *My Cousin Vinnie*.

The Message:

Hey. I just wanted to write real quick to say kudos for picking My Cousin Vinnie as one of your favorite films. For me its always been one of those movies that if I'm channel surfing and come upon it, I just have to watch it.

I noticed that you like hiking and good conversation, two things that I also enjoy. I've been pretty busy of late so haven't gotten a lot of hiking in, but one of my favorite hikes is Neahkahnie Mountain by Manzanita.

I'm also kind of quiet until I get to know people. I guess I'm kind of an introvert with pulses of extrovertism.

Anyways, looking at your profile I thought you might be someone interesting to get to know. Message me back if you'd like.

Shawn

The Result:

I didn't hear anything back. I'm not that surprised. I wouldn't have responded to this message either. I'm a nice guy, blah, blah, blah, nothing interesting. It's the initial messages version of a chain restaurant.

Attempt #37
Mona_Lisas_Spark

Background:

Mona_Lisas_Spark seemed overly proud of the short films she made. Pretty much her entire profile read like it was promotional material. Granted some of the videos were pretty good. I especially liked one that involved farting at a yoga studio which ended with the farter being executed.

The Message:

Hello,
So, I watched some of your videos and found them pretty funny. I did skip some of the longer ones, but it was only because I have to go to bed at a somewhat reasonable hour tonight and I still want to read a chapter or two of my book.

I really enjoyed Yoga Police, TMI, Breakup Blues, and A Peaceful World. I enjoyed Yoga Police because it expresses the fear that keeps me doing yoga in the privacy of my own home. Plus I was impressed with your ability to say the word fart with a completely straight face.

If you want to know why I liked the other ones you'll have to message me back. I believe they call that the hook.

My name is Shawn by the way.

The Result:

Weird, you message somebody and just talk about them, and they message you back. This one actually got to the point where we went out on a date, which went fairly well considering I usually suck at first dates. However, she cancelled the second date the day before it was supposed to happen. It made me a little mad, but I moved on, because that's what reasonable people do.

Attempt #38
Rosecity Rose

Background:

Rosecity Rose's profile didn't have much to go on except for the statement that while she was highly educated she still sometimes forgot which way was right and which way was left.

The Message:

Also being someone who is highly educated but can't seem to ever remember which way is left here is a little trick I learned. Hold both your hands up with your index finger and thumb extended. The one that makes the letter L is left.

I also can't seem to figure out which way should be hot and which way should be cold on a faucet. Though in fairness the house I grew up in had a couple of faucets that worked the wrong way for some reason, so I was kind of screwed from the get go.

My name is Shawn by the way.

The Result:

Not a peep back. Perhaps when she was reading the email she thought I was talking down to her when I was actually only trying to be snarky. I don't know, it's hard to differentiate such things in the written format. Perhaps they need a separate font or something. The thing about the faucets at the house I grew up in is true. To this day my brain is not wired to recognize one side is supposed to be consistently hot and the other consistently cold. I always have to try them out.

Fun fact, the method described to figure out which way is left and which way is right only works if you also know which way the letter L is supposed to be facing. If you don't know that, you're pretty much screwed.

Attempt #39
Aspenpdx

Background:

The process was starting to wear me down again a little bit at this point. I wasn't sending out that many messages and the ones that I did send out were not exactly my Grade A material. I do think the joke I made in this one is pretty funny.

The Message:

Since you like corny jokes, here you go.

Two muffins are baking in the oven. The first muffin says, "man it's hot in here." The second muffin says, "holy shit, a talking muffin!"

I have more, but that was the best one that popped to the top my head. My name is Shawn by the way.

The Result:

Dead silence, every comedian's worst fear. Maybe when she said she liked corny jokes she actually just meant jokes about corn. It's either that or she laughed so hard she had an aneurysm.

On a side note, I'm not sure why I started adding 'my name is Shawn by the way' to a number of these messages. I guess perhaps it gave a more casual tone to the messages, or at the very least made it seem more like an actual conversation rather than a formal letter. It's hard to say. All sorts of crazy shit goes through one's head when they're in their late twenties.

Attempt #40
Illa07

Background:

Illa07's profile had a picture of herself in a top hat. She referred to the top hat as the grandfather of the fedora. Liking both a good analogy (or is it a play on words?) and hats in general, I decided to send her a message.

The Message:

If the top hat is the elegant grandfather of the fedora then is the fedora's father the homburg? Also how does the porkpie hat fit into all of this, is it the fedora's lay about uncle who nobody really likes but still gets invited to family functions? I don't know where to even start with the derby.

My name is Shawn by the way.

The Result:

Nada. I suspect she probably wasn't the hat expert she was trying to make herself out to be.

Attempt #41
Moremingusplz

Background:

At this point my messages slowly started devolving to the point where you couldn't even really call it trying. The string of rejections was starting to sour me to the whole experience.

The Message:

Hi,
By any chance is that Crooked River gorge behind you in your profile picture?

Shawn

The Result:

Unsurprisingly, no. In all fairness she really didn't have much in her profile to go on. Which really brings up the question of why I even bothered to message her. It was because she was attractive, okay, I'm only human.

Given this message was so damn boring, I feel that at least owe you something maybe moderately entertaining. When I was a kid, my parents would often drive on the bridge over Crooked River Gorge. Now for whatever reason, probably related to the fact that my brothers and I tended to be real shits on long car drives, my dad would always tell the story of how a woman had once threw her kids off the bridge whenever we drove on it, a story he'd always end by adding: "Really makes you think doesn't it?"

Attempt #42
Mockmirages

Background:

By this point I was a little bitter which only made things worse. I'm not sure why I kept going at this point other than sheer stubbornness, which certainly didn't help the quality of my initial messages. Reading back over this message I don't know what the hell I was thinking.

The Message:

Damn it. I was going to message you because we both saw Jurassic Park, but I only liked it somewhat. Whelp, too bad.

The Result:

What do you think? Who wouldn't want to go on a date with someone who posts a message like this? On a side note, lots of women seemed to have dinosaur themed names. This one was not one of them, but it was certainly something that I noticed.

Attempt #43
BigfartsLou

Background:

This woman's profile name was BigfartsLou. I don't think I have to explain anything else.

The Message:

Okay, I just have to ask. What's the deal with the screen name?

The Result:

I'm still very curious about the story behind the name.

Attempt #44
Italian237

Background:

There were several noteworthy things about Italian237's profile. First, she stated that she wondered why we all wear clothing. Second, she mentioned that the one thing she could never do without was her frying pan. At this point I had collapsed into mostly just trying to entertain myself.

The Message:

If you wonder why we wear clothes you've probably never caught your genitalia on a thistle while gallivanting naked through a spring meadow.

Also kudos for choosing a frying pan as something you can't do about. A frying pan is a very versatile object. You can cook on it, use it as a weapon if needed, and with the addition of a bit of twine use it as very rudimentary clothing.

The Result:

There's just no impressing some people. You try to work in amazing words like gallivanting into your messages. It's not that easy. Plus, I think I made some very valid points. Then again, perhaps she was bothered by my glaring typo or just thought I was conspiring to steal her precious frying pan.

Attempt #45
Readysetgopanic

Background:

Readysetgopanic stated in her profile that she couldn't get enough meat, didn't like vegan foods, and was into Final Fantasy. Two out of three for me wasn't bad, plus our profile names were reasonably similar, so I decided to just go for it. She was also confused whether the correct nomenclature was 'watching bears fucking' or 'watching bears fuck'. I love wordplay.

The Message:

How's it going. Kudos on your stance concerning vegan cheese. If vegan cheese was so good they wouldn't need to call it vegan cheese, it would have it's own non-cheese related name, like processed soy slices. My apologies for the rant, I just get a little testy when people act like their food choices just won them a nobel prize.

I feel you on the creepy first dates suggestions. I've never gotten those type of offers for a first date, but I once sold a car for $500 or an interesting trade. The offers were quite similar. The only one I regret not taking was the collection of Dale Earnhardt memorabilia.

I would say more but I don't want to ramble on and my knowledge of Japanese RPG's is fairly lacking. My name is Shawn by the way.

P.S. I'm not sure, but my vote would be towards bears fuck.

The Result:

Maybe she meant the other kind of meat, or perhaps a knowledge of Final Fantasy was more important to her than I thought it would be. Either way, I didn't hear anything back. I might have dodged a bullet since there's only so long you can watch bears fuck until you get bored.

On a side note, I highly suggest that any time you sell a cheap car you include the phrase 'or interesting trades considered'. When I sold the Ford Tempo in question in addition to the Dale Earnhardt memorabilia I was offered my pick from a litter of chihuahua puppies, a different shitty car, free cleaning of my house for a month with a heavily implied bonus cleaning of a more personal nature, and a full sized pipe organ. In the end I sold it to a woman for $400 because she had a newborn baby, throwing in the snow tires for free because I felt bad about forgetting to mention that the air conditioning didn't work. All in all, I made a profit on that car, not because of my great sales skills, but rather because it had been in several cosmetic damage causing accidents, all of which I kept the money from rather than getting it fixed.

Attempt #46
DabSlabSolo

Background:

After the long string of failures, I decided to try being normal again, or as normalish as I'm able to fake at any given moment. DabSlabSolo's profile mostly seemed to revolve around how she grew up working in a family business.

The Message:

How's it going? I grew up in a family business as well. My family owns a cattle ranch in Eastern Oregon that my dad and older brother are currently running. That might be why the ad banner on my computer is currently showing Omaha Steaks. Though, now that I think about it, I'm not sure why Google would have that kind of information about me, or really what an ad for Omaha Steaks is doing on a dating website.

Anyways, sorry for the awkward digression. Family businesses, good things. What was the family business you grew up in?

My name is Shawn by the way.

The Result:

Swing and a miss. That might have been a good thing. Looking back over her profile her references to "family business" may have had something to do with "waste management".

Attempt #47
KittyBun

Background:

If I kept the messages short, I could fake being normal. Long messages only led to me giving myself away. Keep it short and to the point. Like many of the online possibles, KittyBun was really into travel. What I said about Asia is absolutely true.

The Message:

If your looking for a new area to travel to, might I suggest Asia. I have been there several times and the best description I can give is that it's the closest thing you can get to going to an alien planet.

My name is Shawn by the way.

The Result:

She was probably going to contact me but got so excited about checking out Asia that she forgot. Yeah, let's go with that.

Reading back over this again, I should probably clarify that Asia seems this way because many countries in it have managed to avoid widespread westernization, maintaining their unique cultures and ways of doing things. A good example of this would be the traditional Chinese focus on avoiding saying no directly. I once spent some time in a Taiwanese bottling factory hearing a hundred different excuses why I shouldn't bother trying to take a picture because they weren't able to outright tell me no.

One trend that I definitely noticed in the online dating world was the focus on travel, sometimes to the point where you wonder if the person thinks that traveling somehow is just as good as being interesting or having a personality. A few other trends I noticed was a lot of women were into rock climbing and many had no compunctions at all about stating very directly that they would not date men shorter than them, the latter of which seems kind of screwed up. I mean, I'm pretty sure if I had put something along the lines of 'no fatties' in my profile I would be a social pariah, even though it's basically the same thing. That being said, I certainly have no qualms in taking advantage of the fact that I'm pretty damn tall. After all, dating is a winner take all kind of world.

Attempt #48
GMoonStruck

Background:

Okay, at this point I was getting a little desperate about the whole thing. I'm fine admitting that. What resulted was something that was probably way too honest for an initial message to a total stranger. I should probably mention that GMoonStruck said she was learning French, hence the ending to prove that I had actually read her profile.

The Message:

Hi,
My name is Shawn. I was looking at your profile and decided to message you, though I guess that part is fairly obvious. I liked the things I read and the pictures I saw. If asked to pinpoint one thing that made me decide to write you I probably could not. Rather, its the entirety of it all together that made me think you would be an interesting person to get to know. I enjoyed your pictures, and not just because you are an attractive woman. I enjoyed the naturally relaxed feeling of them. As well the things

you were doing looked like things I would enjoy doing. I'm curious to know where they were taken.

A little bit about myself. I currently work for a non-profit doing overseas market development work. I enjoy my job even though it has me sitting on my ass more time than I would like. I enjoy running, hiking, anything that gets me outdoors, and seeing things I've never seen before. My main hobby of late has been writing, mostly short stories, though I'm working on a book. I'd like to be published but that still hasn't happened yet, though I enjoy it enough I'd continue writing even if I was never published. Sixty short stories and 60+ rejections so far and I'm still going.

J'espère que vous m'écrivez dos.

Shawn

The Result:

What's that person I've never met before? I probably shouldn't describe word for word my motivations behind messaging you? Yeah, reading back over it, I can see how that was probably pretty weird.

Attempt #49
Lelita02

Background:

Lelita02 seemed to be one of those who tried to convince you she was smart by mentioning obscure names and adding the expectation that no one knows who it is. I'm pretty sure my good sense at weeding such people out was ruined by the constant online rejections I had been experiencing.

The Message:

Touche on the need to wikipedia Alcibiades, though I would like to point out that I googled him. The fact that the first sight to come up was wikipedia was just a coincidence.

I once read an article how scientists discovered microscopic traces of paint on many Greek statues. Their experiments suggested that Ancient Greece, far from being a world of pure white temples and monuments, was more a world of bright clashing colors that even Liberace would call a little much.

I wonder if the people of the Renaissance would have held the Greek world to such an ideal if they had seen the creepy faces painted on the beautiful statues they left behind.

I take your Alcibiades and raise you Zheng He, Hedy Lamarr, and Flavius Aetius.

The Result:

Just so you know, Alcibiades was a famous Ancient Greek statesman, orator, and general from Athens. Also, nobody gives a damn who Alcibiades was.

Attempt #50
BridgesandBeer

Background:

Slowly worn down by rejection, I started abandoning my time-tested method of trying to be funny, replacing it with grasping at any straw I could to try to get some kind of response. Rejection, even online rejection, can wear on you. That being said, some profiles basically wrote the initial messages themselves, while others offered little unique or interesting information and only got messages because I found the person especially attractive. The following message was usually what resulted from the latter, especially when I started getting a little tired of this shit.

The Message:

For Netflix might I suggest House of Cards, though on the lighter side Bob's Burgers is fairly good too.

The Result:

This message even bored me. I'm glad she was not the type of person who would have answered it.

I guess at this point I might as well describe to you how I went about selecting people to message in a bit more detail. Usually when picking people, I first looked at their photos. There were a couple of reasons for this. First, to see if I found them attractive, because it's kind of important, and second, to see if I liked the things they were doing in their photos. Lots of makeup and fancy clothes, negative points. Sporty clothes and goofing around, positive points. If they passed the picture test, I would then read their profiles and try to discern if they were a crazy person and/or someone who looked like a pain in the ass, and any factoids I could use to write a message. However, in all honesty, the majority of profiles pretty much looked the same after going through hundreds of them.

Attempt #51
Afrog8

Background:

Reading back over this message I want to invent a time machine, go back in time, and punch myself in the face. I have no idea what I was thinking. I'm not sure how I suddenly turned into Reginald P. Boringuy III.

The Message:

Welcome to Portland. In my humble opinion it's the best city on the West Coast, though in all fairness I might be a little biased. It is probably the first city I've lived in where I haven't had the desperate feeling to move somewhere else.

I enjoyed the part of your profile about about time being more important than money. I think that too often people forget that money is just a representation of time they've given away. While I believe in living comfortably, the number of days off I get seems just as important as what I get paid.

Anywho, I'm always looking for people to go do fun things with that seem like they would be interesting to be around. Maybe get a drink and catch a show or something along those lines. Cheers.

Shawn

The Result:

Hmmmm…. what's that extremely boring message? You didn't illicit a response? Well, that's weird.

Attempt #52
Purple_Tango

Background:

With this next message I at least tried to return to my roots of coming up with an original message that would both entertain and titillate. I probably went a little overboard in that most women don't like it when strangers accuse them of jihad.

The Message:

I do not think it's right for you to declare chicken has no place on pizza. I'll grant you that chicken on pizza is dry, tasteless, and just plain terrible. However, I would like to think we live in a world where all meats have an equal chance of ending up on pizza according to the eaters choice. Personally, I would never order chicken on pizza, even if it was the only thing on the menu, but I'm also not declaring a public wide pizza on chicken jihad either, like some people.

On a side note I can de-bone a chicken at record speeds. I'm not saying that I've won any international chicken de-boning contests, but I'm also not denying that I may have come in second place.

The Result:

All quiet from this one. It's probably for the best. She obviously had some kind of meat bias (meatism?). She was also probably intimidated by my chicken deboning skills.

Attempt #53
Pj68

Background:

There were a few things that stood out about Pj68's profile. First, she was involved in competitive log rolling. Second, she was constantly wondering how to avoid having to deal with automated answering machines.

The Message:

Personally my strategy to get straight to live operators is to constantly hit the 0 or 9 button until the computer gives up in its attempt to communicate with me. While I know it's not the way it works, I like to imagine some kind of robot on the other end belching smoke and saying the word "error" repeatedly. If you have a different method I would be glad to hear it.

Also, competitive log roller. Awesome.

The Result:

Nothing. I don't think she was actually looking for dates, just new ideas on how to get to real operators when dealing with automated answering systems. On a side note, my strategy does work. Feel free to use it.

Attempt #54
Zomozoo

Background:

Zomozoo's profile mentioned that she was moderately good at faking accents. I kind of latched on to that and then ran with it. Like most things I run with, I probably carried it way too far and shared way too much. The message soon became large and unwieldy.

The Message:

I am also a moderate expert at faking accents, though often times they seem to morph into a British accent without rhyme or reason. My most famous performance to date was when I first moved to Portland five years ago.

I had only recently moved to town and after a few months of sitting around I finally met a group of nice, and mostly normal, people to hang out with. They invited me to go bar hopping downtown so I jumped on the Max to join them, realizing only upon exiting at my destination that I had forgotten my phone at home.

Unperturbed I joined my new comrades at the first bar and, like a bear emerging from hibernation, proceeded to gorge myself on libations at a much quicker than planned on pace. This over indulgence, while loosening my tongue, also wrecked my attention span. I was almost left behind at several bars due to my own inattention, and one new friend, concerned, wrote their phone number on my hand in case I should become lost.

This proved to be a wise move because soon after, I looked up from a conversation I was having with some random bar fly, to discover everyone I knew had gone. I'm pretty sure someone had told me where they were going, but in my cloudy state I plum forgot. I rushed out on the street, but much to my chagrin, my compatriots were nowhere in sight.

Still having some of my mental faculties I remembered the phone number on my hand and proceeded to ask other pedestrians if I could borrow their phones. Despite Portland's reputation, this did not go well, possibly due to my high state of inebriation. After the third rejection, dejected and unsure, I had a genius moment.

The next person I stopped to make my request I did so using an Irish accent that would be considered passable if you had worked your entire life in an aircraft hangar and had never met anyone from Ireland before. This amazingly enough worked. Unfortunately no one answered when I made the call.

I was disappointed at still being lost, but the amazement at the difference an accent made far overshadowed it. I was so impressed with my new found knowledge that I used it on about five other people just to make sure it wasn't a fluke. Every time the phone was handed over without question. I never found my friends again that night, but I did ride the Max home with a feeling that it had been a good night.

The Result:

The above story is entirely true. Unfortunately, it apparently was not impressive enough to score me a message back. Fortunately, I have the power to borrow strangers' phones at will, so there's that at least.

Attempt #55
Ladysassyfras

Background:

Ladysassyfrass mentioned that she had recently learned the difference between a shank and a shiv, which struck me as a little weird, but I ran with it. After a little Googling research, I was surprised to learn there is actually quite a bit of debate on these two pieces of prison nomenclature.

The Message:

Reading your profile I hit the part about shank and shiv and instantly thought of this.

Prisoner 1: Ha, shanked you bitch.

Prisoner 2: I'm pretty sure you mean shivved.

Prisoner 1: Hey, I didn't spend all this time sharpening my toothbrush to have you question my nomenclature.

Prisoner 2: I think a shank has to be made of metal.

Prisoner 1: That doesn't sound right. I'm pretty sure a shank involves stabbing while a shiv involves cutting.

Prisoner 2: That's silly. The words are identifying objects, not actions.

Prisoner 1: Yes, but the words for the actions are directly derived from the words for the objects.

Prisoner 2: Granted, but I still disagree with the assertion that you can't stab someone with a shiv.

Prisoner 3: Actually you're both right. A shiv is any knife-like object while a shank is a homemade knife.

(Prisoner 1 and 2 stare at Prisoner 3 blankly).

Prisoner 3: So therefore, a shank is a type of shiv.

(Prisoner 1 and 2 look at each other. Prisoner 1 stabs Prisoner 3)

Prisoner 1: Shut up ya know it all.

Prisoner 2: I guess he got shivved and shanked.

Prisoner 1: Damn straight.

Prisoner 2: Glad we got that cleared up. Would you mind helping me to the infirmary. I've lost a lot of blood.

Anyways, this is usually how my mind works. Long convoluted stories out of little statements. Also nice choice on Bob's Burgers. Awesome show.

The Result:

If I got a message like this, I probably wouldn't answer either.

Attempt #56
Cdgb

Background:

In her list of skills, Cdgb stated that she knew how to escape from a helicopter that crashed into the ocean. I'm not really sure how one learns something like this. So many questions. Either way I thought that this was a pretty creative message. As a side note, she also claimed to have a weird middle name.

The Message:

I would be very interested in hearing any advice on how to escape from a helicopter crashing into the ocean. The engine is smoking profusely now and I'm pretty sure we're not going to make the shoreline.

I probably got a few more minutes. I'm sure a fellow dim sum fan such as yourself will help me out. I just hope I get through this so I can enjoy at least one more Sunday morning at Wong Kings.

I know it might seem a little strange given my current predicament, but I must admit that I am strangely curious to know what your middle name is. It can't be half as embarrassing as mine.

The Result:

Nada. Personally, I think if I got a message like this I would answer, just on the off chance that somebody really was in a crashing helicopter. I should probably admit that my middle name is not weird at all, I was just trying to weasel hers out of her. I enjoy a good mystery.

Attempt #57
Rodbot

Background:

Rodbot was looking specifically for creative dating ideas. I don't know if my idea was really all that creative, but it sure the hell was awesome.

The Message:

Wait for it......what about breakfast for dinner. That's right, I'm talking about brinner. The most magical meal ever to be created. We're talking about waffles and syrup in the dark of night. We're talking about sunny side eggs under the light of the moon. We're talking mother fuckin' french toast with a side of bourbon. There is nothing better in this world, or more relaxing, than brinner.

Also in answer to your question, yes, it is all right to binge drink on the weekend. There is probably no more socially acceptable time period to consume mass quantities of inebriates.

The Result:

Surprisingly no. Who the hell doesn't like brinner? Brinner is the most awesome meal in the history of people sitting down to eat. If you want romance, you need to try having brinner with your lucky companion.

Attempt #58
CtotheClay

Background:

CtotheClay hated baseball announcers and was an expert caulker. It was hard to not take this one too far. I think the long string of rejections was starting to get to me at this point, which resulted in a fairly direct ending.

The Message:

So, your good at caulking. Some low brow unclassy people would probably use that as the basis for a terrible line of jokes which would be entirely inappropriate to put in an initial message, but not me. Nope, I'm above all that. Plus none of the jokes I thought of were really all that funny.

Switching directions away from my poorly thought out caulking comments, personally I feel bad for baseball announcers. They constantly have to strive to find something interesting to say while at the same time knowing that nobody really gives a damn. They just have to sit in a little box with the color commentator, who gets to make witty comments, while they desperately look up stats on how many times the guy up to bat has struck out versus southpaw pitcher's on a Tuesday night.

Anyways, that's enough crazy ranting to try and stand out. My name is Shawn. I'm driven and goal oriented. I have a good job and own my own home. I'm constantly trying to make myself a better and more rounded person. I'm looking to meet new and interesting people who have realistic expectations. I'm being fairly direct here at the end because you seem like the kind of person who would respect that, plus I enjoy soaking in hot tubs and it seems like you have a few to spare. I hope to hear back from you.

The Result:

And at last, the losing streak was broken. I got a message back from her calling me a nut, but in a good way. We messaged back and forth a few times and tried to set up a date, but nothing ever came of it.

Attempt #59
Lizzy_Pants

Background:

Two things that stood out in Lizzy_Pants' profile. One was a reference to missing the show *Breaking Bad.* The other was some kind of joke about only being able to know what she did on Friday nights if you were hiding in her linen closet, because she spent her Fridays at home apparently.

The Message:

How's it going? I apologize for being in your linen closet. I do not have a linen closet at my house. I just have a closet full of camping supplies and board games, which make my closet very uncomfortable to skulk in.

There, now that I've done my level best to make this initial message awkward as hell I can talk about more normal things. Like how the pumpkins in your profile are segregated by color. It makes me sad that the mixing of varieties is still frowned upon in the world of pumpkins.

Darn it. That was just as awkward as the first one. Oh well. Gone too far to turn back now. Hopefully you found some of my odd sense of humor funny. If not, I do know a fairly good joke involving muffins. My name is Shawn by the way.

P.S. Saw this video just the other day referencing people missing Breaking Bad. Figured from your profile you could use it.

The Result:

Amazingly enough this worked, even though I forgot to include the video referencing people missing *Breaking Bad.* She even had a witty remark about her being the Strom Thurmond of pumpkins. Unfortunately, this was another situation where we messaged back and forth a lot but could never get our calendars to match up. Though this might be a good thing, given now that I think about it, the Strom Thurmond comment might have been a bit of a red flag.

Attempt #60
GMoonStruck

Background:

One of the more interesting things I noticed while online dating on and off over a significant period of time was the number of times you would start to see the same person. You'd get off for a while, get back on, or they'd disappear, and then re-appear, but again and again similar faces would pop up, giving a strange comfort in that I wasn't the only one failing to find love. Even stranger was when some of these faces became familiar enough that I began to notice them out in public. There they would be, a person I had a strangely large amount of knowledge about given the profiles of the time but had never once interacted with other than possibly a message or two. I actually later became friends with a few of these people through random happenstance, though of course I never mentioned that I recognized them, because that would just be plain weird.

Regarding this specific message, it was actually to the same GMoonStruck as Attempt #48. At some point a friend had told me that women get so many messages that it was easy to get swept under the rug and forgotten about, so there was nothing wrong with waiting a month or two and then sending a second message. I tried to do a better job on this message, but her profile didn't really have a lot to work with.

The Message:

I'm no expert on these things, but it seems your living your life a bit on the edge. I'm judging this entirely based upon the fact that you like to be outside a lot, but yet have no sense of direction.

On the plus side, being lost somewhere in the middle of nowhere, or just possibly in Forest Park, still beats sitting at a desk all day.

The Result:

This would probably have worked better if the messaging system on the online dating site I was using didn't instantly show the weird message I'd sent a month ago above the new message I had just sent. All in all, I probably shouldn't have listened to my friend, especially given they were the same one who suggested I just send hello to everyone instead of wasting my time on elaborate initial messages.

Attempt #61
MegaTrashThree

Background:

MegaTrashThree claimed she had impeccable posture. She also stated that she only wanted to date adults, which is a good thing, since dating children is illegal. I like to stay pretty open minded, but that's a hard no for me. She also stated that she was very stubborn and never changed her mind. Looking back, I have no idea why I messaged this woman.

The Message:

Good posture is important, nobody likes a sloucher. Of course, before I believe your claim I'd have to see you walk from one end of the bar to the other with a beer on your head. It's not that posture is a deal breaker, I just like to see people back up what they say.

I would say I'm an adult when I have to be an adult. What I am the rest of the time is really my business. By adult I mean someone who is independent and lives within their own means, knows how to communicate and express themselves in a healthy manner, and doesn't have unrealistic expectations based upon somebody else or the world owing them for anything.

I can be a stubborn jack ass but don't hold on to my opinions just because they're mine. If someone can make a good point that proves me wrong I'll change my opinion. I should probably underline the word good in that last sentence.

I'm willing to bet I can teach you new things. For instance, the best Chinese food in town is at Wong Kings on Division. If you already know that I do know other things as well.

My name is Shawn by the way.

The Result:

Not so much. However, if you've never been to Wong King's for Sunday breakfast I do highly suggest going. Be sure to arrive around 9:30 or 10:00 so you can beat the huge crowds of Chinese people who eat there. Though of course you'll also have to buy a time machine to go there, given it's been closed since the pandemic, so yeah, good luck with that.

Attempt #62
HifiveNHugs

Background:

This profile didn't have a lot to work with, but HifiveNHugs seemed like a very nice woman, so I decided to give it the old college try. By this time, I had again firmly entrenched the idea that I needed to make people laugh in order to get them to notice me.

The Message:

Nobody is going to judge you for watching Glee. However, people are definitely going to judge you for singing and dancing along with the numerous snazzy dance numbers, possibly while wearing a homemade clumsily bedazzled outfit.

Hello by the way, my name is Shawn.

The Result:

It worked. I took it slow with this one and let several messages go back and forth before, apparently getting tired of my dilly-dallying, she asked me out. We went on a couple dates and had a fairly good time all things considered, but in the end we both didn't feel that spark that we were looking for. In the end, we mutually agreed to look elsewhere, wishing each other luck in our respective searches.

Attempt #63
Kittymeowmeow

Background:

I kind of only messaged Kittymeowmeow because her profile had some things I could work with and one of her pictures showed that she had a pretty nice ass. Actually, to be honest, that's probably how I picked out most of the women I messaged.

The Message:

What exactly constitutes too much animal print? Personally I think unless your wardrobe is starting to resemble the closet of Cruella DeVille or the baggage train of an old timey Big Game hunting safari you probably don't have too much to worry about.

You should probably also consider the possibility that perhaps the animal print might be aiding your legendary kitten taming prowess. It's been awhile since I tamed any kittens myself, I was once pretty good at it, so I'm not 100% up on my young feline psychology, but I imagine a vaguely cat like appearance can only help the process.

Of course if you ever find yourself wearing animal print and thinking that maybe furry fetishist are on to something, then you should probably just light your closet on fire immediately.

My name is Shawn by the way.

The Result:

Amazingly enough, I got a response back. Which is pretty impressive considering I suggested she burn her entire wardrobe. We messaged back and forth for a while but never set up a date that worked for both of us. I'm okay with that, I'm not sure if I want to be seen in public with someone who wears a lot of animal print.

Attempt #64
Crescentmoony37

Background:

This message just burst out of my mind in its complete form. Without even bothering to towel it off I pushed it out into the world to see what would happen. Out of all my messages, this one was probably the most faithful to how my mind works on a day-to-day basis.

The Message:

I noticed in your profile that your looking for new partners in crime. That's perfect because I've been planning the crime of the century and I need a second person for the job.

This job is going to require some muscle and a femme fatale. I'm up for being either but you have to choose one well before the job so I can either hit the gym or go to a day spa. All we'll need is a wrench, two slim jims, a tube of cherry chapstick, and two extremely ridiculous looking wigs. Your also going to need to falsify your dental records in case we have to fake our own deaths to avoid the fuzz. I'm not going to lie to you, there is a definite risk of prison time.

The target is the Electric Castle Wunderland arcade. Old man Wunder is loaded.

First step is to go in and play several rounds of air hockey, because I'll be damned if I go into that place and not play air hockey.

Second the femme fatale will go to the skee ball machines and after playing a bit will loudly start throwing a fit and yelling that they're short on balls.

Third, while security is distracted the muscle will go to those machines where you try to push nickels off a shelf using other nickels and give them a good shake, resulting in a king's ransom worth in tickets.

Fourth, we take the tickets and buy ourselves the most lucrative prizes available. The model ship with a clock in it, several spider rings, a stuffed pink panther, and a plastic whistle.

Fifth, we fence our loot on e-bay, netting tens of dollars.

Sixth, we flee to Rio, leaving Kevin to be the fall guy.

Seventh, we drink mai tais.

It's a flawless plan. So, you in?

The Result:

I didn't get a message back for some time. She was on vacation apparently. The message I did get back involved the phrase, "holy awesomeness Batman" which is about the best complement one can get. We went on a date, and it seemed pretty damn good overall, at least at first.

The Third Hiatus

I'm not going to lie to you, which is a bit of a strange phrase when you think about it, I mean, c'mon, does that mean I'm lying to you all the rest of the time? Anyways, I'm not going to lie to you, things got weird. How weird you ask? Really weird. So weird that I wrote a whole short story about it. What happened? Well, that's not really important right now. I guess if you really want to know you could find out via the short story *Probably Crazy* in my short story collection *Stumptown*. What's that you say, an advertisement for a different book right in the middle of this book? That's right mother fuckers, it's called capitalism. Get used to it. Please feel free to insert an evil laugh here, or even better, loudly do your evil laugh, especially if you're on the bus or some other public setting.

Anyways, at this point I decided that it was probably best to take a little break to give a bit of thought about the ins and outs of my attraction to people who were a bit more unhinged compared to the average person. As a result, I didn't online date for about two months.

Attempt #65
DanaZee86

Background:

I was a little more nervous about crazy this time around. Having accepted that I was attracted to crazy, I was doing my level best to try and avoid it as much as possible. DanaZee86 seemed nice. She said she was good at parallel parking and needed a good peanut butter bread recipe. I was nervous, so of course random shit got sent.

The Message:

A woman who can parallel park, well I'll be. To be honest, I'm terrible at parallel parking so I guess the world is just full of gender bending these days.

Of course, your parking abilities are probably just because you're from Ohio, something which I don't hold entirely against you since I already know several people of the same unfortunate upbringing. I find it strange that people from every other eastern and Midwestern state came to Oregon on the Oregon Trail, while

Ohio people are just coming now. But I guess being 150 years behind schedule is just par for the course.

Oh, and by the way. I've added a link to a pretty good peanut butter bread recipe. Your welcome.

The Result:

Reading this again, it's probably not the best to start a message with a gender stereotype and then insult somebody's state of origin. The fact that I forgot to include the peanut butter recipe link definitely didn't help either.

Attempt #66
Anna9285

Background:

I'm pretty sure I only sent this message because her profile was written like it was a challenge. Want to date me? Good luck. Nobody is good enough. I do not do well against challenges. My default is to prove the person wrong. I once ate a three-pound bowl of ice cream just because the lady at the counter off-handedly mentioned that I probably wouldn't be able to do it.

The Message:

Intimidated by your announcement that you probably won't respond since you don't really want to be here, I have endeavored to do my best to garner a return message.

I not only know the difference between there, their, and they're, but also thar. The last one is only used if you're an old timey pirate.

I am taller than you, a good four inches taller. You could wear heels. If you want to wear higher than four inch heels I could probably wear some lifts. We could tromp around like a pair of Godzilla's, laughing down at the tiny people.

I as well have excellent posture. I do not have steel rods in my spine, so you have me on that one. My posture is rather due to the fear of being one of those tall people you see all stooped over.

I love the outdoors. Last weekend I went on a ten mile hike along the old Tillamook railroad across trestles and through tunnels. I killed a wolverine with my bare hands. Part of this paragraph is not true.

I don't give a god damn Jesus loving fart about blasphemy.

If I was any happier with who I am I'd probably be illegal. I'm getting high on my own supply, of life that is.

I'm as healthy as a horse, assuming of course, that the horse in question is itself pretty damn healthy. No ma'am, no sickly horse like people over here.

My name is Shawn by the way. Nice to meet you.

The Result:

This profile was taken down soon after I sent this message. I like to think that after reading my message she realized that she could never be good enough for me and gave up dating to join a nunnery. Go me.

Attempt #67
Ardvark318

Background:

This woman really liked Paul Rudd, as in she mentioned his name somewhere around four times in her profile. However, I did not let my lack of Paul Ruddness deter me.

The Message:

I was once told that I look like Paul Rudd, but that was by a Korean man who soon after admitted that all Americans look the same to him. So yeah, I don't really look like Paul Rudd.

Unlike you, I have used a porta-potty, an experience that I would describe as less then satisfactory, but sufficient given the alternative of ruining my favorite pair of pants.

I am a fan of the Sopranos pinball machine, but I like the Medieval Madness one better.

My name is Shawn by the way.

The Result:

If they can't even handle using a porta-potty, they probably aren't going to be able to handle my lifestyle. Not getting a message back was probably for the best.

As an aside, I actually was once told by a Korean coworker that I looked like Paul Rudd, but this was in the middle of him giving me a shoulder rub, which I was told is a perfectly normal thing to do to one's coworkers in Korea. Given this, and the fact that he told me all white people look alike to him, I'm fairly doubtful of the accuracy of his claim.

Attempt #68
Mollyjp12

Background:

Mollyjp12's profile highlighted that was sick and tired of people setting up dates only to reveal later that they had some little ones hidden in the wings. She must have been one of those DIY people.

The Message:

Hi, my name is Shawn.

I wouldn't worry too much about not knowing how to ski or snowboard. I am person that shares a similar quality, or lack thereof depending on how you think about it. I grew up out in the middle of the desert so taking up the whitest sport known to man was never much of an option.

I don't have any kids, at least as far as I know, but who knows, given your past dating experience maybe just writing this message will be enough to pop one out of the wood work. I hope not, but I guess those are the breaks.

Anyways, that's probably enough weirdness for one initial message to someone I've never met before. Write back if you'd like.

The Result:

Maybe she thought I meant a baby popping out of her woodwork when I made that joke. That's a well-used euphemism, right?

Attempt #69
Anu444

Background:

A friend told me about a really creative online dating message they got where the guy pretended that he was ending the relationship. I thought it was hilarious, so of course I stole the shit out of it. Plus, given my history of dating, getting ahead of the curve seemed like a good idea.

The Message:

I'm sorry, but I think it's time we end this farce. It's over. I can't take it anymore. The constant fighting over frozen yogurt vs. frozen custard. You always eating all of the cheese. You getting mad at me every Passover for smearing lamb's blood over our doorway. I'm sorry, it has all just become too much.

You can have it all. The house, the kids, our strangely eclectic collection of acoustic albums, and that horrendous lamp you insisted we get at that yard sale last year. All I'm taking is our vintage Ford Ranchero and our cat Dr. Pickles. He always liked me better anyways.

I wish you the best. I hope you understand.

Shawn

The Result:

There are just some women out there who won't take the risk, no matter how handsome you are, of losing their vintage Ford Ranchero.

Attempt #70
BrighterQuicker

Background:

One thing that happens from time to time when you online date enough is that you begin perusing profiles you've already perused before without realizing it until you go to message them. Usually I don't bother, but in this specific case, for whatever reason, I decided to say fuck it and just send a message anyways. For reference, this was the same person as Attempt #14.

The Message:

So, funny story. I recently reactivated my OkCupid account and started perusing the options out there as one is wont to do when part of such internet based socializing. I came upon your profile, and finding myself interested, decided to send you a message.

This is the part where it takes a twist. You seemed familiar. My sense of deja vu was justified when I went to hit the message button, a low and behold, sure enough, you were someone that I went on a date with two years ago. If memory serves me right a second one was later cancelled, under the reason of getting back with an ex, though in all fairness that may have been an indirect brushoff on your part as sometimes happens.

This left me in a quandary since I remember that I did enjoy the date, or at least as much as anyone can when they meet someone for the first time. However, it seemed risky to send this message, given that it might be construed as weird.

In the end I decided to send it anyways, because if you don't fish you never catch, and at worst somebody I'll probably never see again will think I'm weird, which isn't so bad considering most of my closest friends probably think the same.

In conclusion. Hello. How are you?

The Result:

For the first time in this round of online dating I got a message back. Point for me. The message went something like this, “oh yeah, I remember that date, I had a lot of fun, it was great, never contact me again you creepy bastard.” So, I guess point rescinded.

Attempt #71
Noctiflora

Background:

What the hell is a sand ball? This was the most pertinent thing on my mind, yet I didn't have the guts to ask. Instead let's just talk about random bullshit and completely ignore the elephant in the room.

The Message:

Hi, my name is Shawn, consider me intrigued.

I don't know much about sand balls, but I have made some pretty epic drip castles before. My brother and I also once built a large sand dam across a small creek and flooded half a beach one time. But it was totally okay since it was "completely" only to entertain my niece who was two at the time.

Right now I'm sitting in a hotel room in Omaha, waiting to go through meetings for the next couple days so I can come home to Portland. Don't know why that's pertinent, but it seems to be the main thing on my mind right now.

I am one of the few people left who does not have a smart phone. This is the case for several reasons, but one of the main ones is because it allows me to still get lost from time to time.

Anyway, hope to hear back from you.

The Result:

I will never get to know what a sand ball is. This is something I will have to live with for the rest of my life. Oh, the regret. On the plus side, that day on the beach with my niece was easily in my top ten good days so far.

Attempt #72 TwoMuddyBoots

Background:

Things were not going well on this go around. Not only was I not getting any dates, I wasn't even getting any return messages. Was it me? Probably. Was I being too weird? Most likely. Maybe I needed to turn it down a notch. You know, ease them into my world.

The Message:

Hi, my name is Shawn. Nice to meet you.

I enjoy the outdoors as well, though this seems to be something that everyone in Portland shares. Last week I went on a nice hike on the abandoned Tillamook Railroad, through a few tunnels and across a couple trestles. This week I'm in Omaha for work, so I took a nice run along the Missouri River. Been on any good hikes lately?

I'm never sure what to write for these initial messages. It always seems hard to stand out. So I guess I'll do what I'd do if this was in person.

Work once sent me to Japan, and since it was a long trip, sent me their first class. It was a very early flight, so I was very tired, but still excited since I had never flown first class before. I sat down in my seat, and amazed by the myriad of controls, started punching them to put my seat in a more relaxing position. They didn't work. A fact that really annoyed me since the person across the aisle had their seat in full recline. After playing with the controls more I finally looked up and figured out why my seat controls weren't working. I was actually messing with my neighbors seat controls. She was a very elderly Japanese lady. It was a very awkward flight.

Well, that's all I got. Hope to hear back from you.

The Result:

Hmmmm.... turns out Normal Shawn isn't any more successful than Weird Shawn. Good to know. The great return message drought continued.

Attempt #73
Ilikestuff196

Background:

I think I just kind of lost it here. I was still trying to be in Normal Shawn mode, but I think I was tired of writing messages that got no responses. I don't think I ever really got bitter, but there's only so many rejections you can take before you get a bit frustrated.

The Message:

Hello,
Wait....you like traveling, doing stuff, enjoying a good drink, and not eating directly out of cans? That's a weird coincidence. I also enjoy the majority of these things (the last largely depends on the contents of the can). I especially noted your fandom of food. I am also a big fan of food. In fact, I partake of it several times a day. We seem to have a lot in common.

After reviewing my profile pictures I am sorry to report that I do have one selfie. However, it should be pointed out that my shirt is on, I'm not in front of a mirror, it was National Tiara Day, and the 70 year old secretary I was working with was feeling a little blue. The reason it is up on my profile is because a friend who likes to play tricks on me convinced me it would be a good idea to put it up, and to take it down now would be to admit that they got me, something that is not going to happen. Plus it allows me to relate that story, which is more effective then just saying that I'm a nice guy.

Anyhow, hope to hear back from you. Maybe put a reminder for yourself on a post-it. This is one you do not want to miss.

Ciao.

P.S. My name is Shawn by the way.

The Result:

Fun fact. Vomiting facts about yourself and similarities between the two of you all over someone's lap rarely gets them to talk to you. Second fun fact. A person only has so much suave in them in a given month and mine had run dry by this point.

Attempt #74
Tittypryde

Background:

My energy was depleted. My ability to offer more than two, or even one, fucks was completely gone. I regret to say that I dropped to a new low in online dating initial messaging. I re-used an initial message. It was too easy, and the original had been written years ago. I know, no excuse. I'm so ashamed.

The Message:

Since you may or may not have a apocalypse survival kit ready to go, I feel like you're someone who would appreciate that I have a full apocalypse escape plan. If year's of watching public service announcements has taught me anything, it's be prepared.

My apocalypse escape plans involves an armored bus carrying at least 15 survivors with very mismatched personalities to the area of the state with the lowest population density. I envision it to be a combination of MTV's Road Rules and the Road Warrior. I estimate that in our journey at least 5 people will die, 3 being minor characters, 1 being a major douchebag who betrays the group in some way, and 1 being the most skilled character who has shown the most heroism and wisdom during the journey. When we build our new utopian city, we will name it after him/her.

The Result:

Nope. In my mind I imagine there is a weekly meeting of women who are interested in the apocalypse or the end of the world. For some reason it always devolves to talking about the hot dudes that send them online dating messages. One brings up my message, another states she got the same one a few years ago. They both laugh at how unimaginative I must be and how I would be no help at the end of the world. Survival requires creativity.

Attempt #75
Mhhh5

Background:

I'm pretty sure I completely lost my mind at this point. This, my fourth attempt at online dating, had resulted in nothing but silence. Was I really that undatable? Did I just have the worst luck known to man? No more trying to be suave, no more being funny, no more being cute, I went into full on 'Used Car Salesman' mode.

The Message:

Intentional spontaneity, now that is something that I would have to see to believe. Hi, my name is Shawn. I was reading through your profile and liked what I saw. While I do not have dual citizenship, I did live in Canada for a year. Unfortunately, except for the one hidden in my profile pictures, I can't think of any Canada jokes off the top of my head.

I'm never really sure what to write in these messages, but since you seem to be someone who knows what you want, I guess I'll just put some fun facts about myself and see what happens.

Most of my artistic passion is towards writing. I've written a heap of short stories and after a hundred or so rejections I'm finally getting one published. I'm now working on getting more out there. I'm also about halfway through a novel, though this keeps getting delayed because I get distracted writing short stories.

I also enjoy taking photographs. I've gotten a couple published and in the future plan on putting more effort into getting them out there.

I enjoy long drives down roads I've never been on before and hiking. Recently I drove up Highway 1 around Big Sur and then spent a day in San Francisco. Recently I also took an interesting hike on the abandoned Tillamook Railroad across several old trestles and through several tunnels.

My goal this summer has been to try and increase my culture. I sat in the third row of the Pirates of the Penzance and I'm going to two chamber music concerts this month.

I'm a voracious reader. I'm currently reading Islands In The Stream. Recently I read One Hundred Years of Solitude, Sometimes A Great Notion, and The Rum Diary.

I work a good job that I enjoy and am in a good place financially. I own my own home.

I enjoy my life immensely.

Anyways, again, not sure if this is the best way to go about this. I usually try to make jokes and the such. I put a bunch of them together once and got them put on a website. But, overall it didn't work out so well, so now I'm going with the overly direct approach.

So in summary, from reading your profile you seem like somebody I would like to meet. If after reading all this and looking at my profile you feel the same, let me know. Cheers

The Result:

Of course it was a no. Nobody wants to read a huge ass message that reads like a resume. The only thing I failed to include were my healthcare records. You smell that stink. That my friends is desperation.

Attempt #76
SunshineStream

Background:

I had fallen so far that there was only one way to go, back up. Not that the messages suddenly became amazing, but at least I put a little bit of effort back into them again. If I was going to go down, I was going to go down swinging. SunshineStream's profile mentioned how she loved Scrabble and had the habit of kicking down doors. I'm not sure why I wrote this message in the third person, let's just assume I was drunk.

The Message:

Shawn enjoyed reading Sunshine Stream's profile and thinks she seems like an interesting person. He was somewhat concerned for the safety of his doors, but decided what the hell, life is full of risks.

Despite Sunshine Stream's claim of being a worthy scrabble opponent, Shawn still feels like he could beat. This is not because Shawn has a larger vocabulary, he most likely doesn't, but because is a master at adding to other people's words to make them past tense or plural.

Shawn looks forward to hearing back from Sunshine Stream.

The Result:

Nada. However, I did create a new rule for myself. No more giving away my winning Scrabble strategies until at least the third date. Also, again, third person, what the hell?! I swear to god I was drunk.

Attempt #77
Lost_girlscout

Background:

This potential gal pal mentioned that she often worked her balls off. I always found this a funny turn of phrase for a woman.

The Message:

I always find it funny when women refer to working their balls off. Personally I think we need to come up with some gender specific euphemism for women to use in such cases of hard work. After doing some brainstorming on this end, I've come up with the following:

"Working my ovaries out."

I'm open to better suggestions, but if there are none, then I suggest we contact the American Society of Phrasing immediately to get this registered.

My name is Shawn by the way.

The Result:

Nothing, but it didn't matter. The message was back up to my standards. I was back baby, and better than ever. Okay, maybe not better than ever, but you get the idea. With all that said, I should probably check with the American Society of Phrasing to make sure she didn't take credit for my idea.

Attempt #78
Awk_Emily

Background:

I wasn’t even sure why I was still going. Probably just pure stubbornness at this point. Always finding new and creative ways to write initial messages was slowly sucking my brain dry. I needed to throw one last desperate haymaker, one last Hail-Mary pass.

The Message:

I couldn't help but notice that your drinking a glass of white wine in the forest in one of your profile pics. Not to be judgmental, but seriously, what were you thinking? Everyone knows that red wines go with deciduous forests. White wines go best with conifers.

Also, this is completely out of left field, but I'm guessing that your upstairs neighbor vacuums after midnight because they have filthy dreams. This results in them feeling so dirty that they have to clean everything in their house. Just a guess.

The Result:

Success. After shouting into the void for longer than I cared to remember, an answer came floating back, a witty one to boot. It seemed like some kind of miracle. However, after only one return message she disappeared back from whence she came, into the depths of the web, but for a moment, for just a moment, I tasted victory, and my thirst was slaked.

Attempt #79
PizzaXperiment

Background:

Refreshed and reinvigorated, I started back out on my quest to see what the online dating world had to offer. I was still a little cocky from my recent victory, so I probably got a little overconfident on this one.

The Message:

I'm a little disturbed by the fact that you can include George Jones and Johnny Cash in your list of old country stars, but not include Merle Haggard. Though perhaps that's just me.

Hi, my name is Shawn. Looked at your profile, liked what I saw, figured I send a message.

I'm a fan of Fitzgerald, though to be honest, I can't figure out whether he or his wife was the crazier one. I must admit that I'm a bit biased due to reading Hemingway's opinion on the subject. However, to be fair, you read enough Hemingway it becomes pretty obvious that he was eventually going to off himself, so maybe his is not the best opinion to base my judgement on.

Well, that's a weird tangent. Anyways, message me back if you'd like and the above hasn't weirded you out too much.

The Result:

Silence. Back to the norm. In retrospect it probably isn’t the best idea to mention suicidal authors when you introduce yourself. Yeah, definitely not a good idea.

Attempt #80
Findyourbliss

Background:

I decided to go with a slightly different tact with this one. Humor wasn't working, so how about blunt honesty. This is overall usually what I look for in women, though I have been known to make exceptions from time to time.

The Message:

To be honest I nearly passed your profile by just because you didn't have much information in it. However, while looking over the slim pickings I did notice that in your second picture you had a significant amount of back sweat. I have to tell you, I've done a lot of perusing on this sight, looked at a lot of profiles, and you don't see many women with pictures like that. I have one word for you. Awesome.

So there you go. A message simply because you are not afraid to hide the fact that your body behaves in the way it would be expected to during rigorous exertion. I hope to hear back from you, but either way mystery woman with the back sweat pic, my hat is off to you.

The Result:

The good. She responded back. Not only that, but she was familiar with the Hash House Harriers. The bad. She knew who I was, calling me by my hash name and everything, while I on the other hand had absolutely no memory of her. The ugly. I tried to pretend that I did indeed remember her. I was unsuccessful.

Attempt #81
PizzaXperiment

Background:

This attempt represented a new low. As I've previously stated, a friend once told me that women get so many messages that it's totally acceptable to send them another message if they don't respond, advice which had not panned out for me at all the first two times I had tried to apply it. Given this, I'm not really sure why I decided to try it again, or more concerning, why I thought it was a good idea to try it again on someone who I had so recently messaged. There must have been something especially eye catching in PizzaXperiment's profile. Hello again Miss Attempt #79.

The Message:

Question. Why do you take all your pictures in the same corner of your house? Not really judging. Just scientific curiosity.

The Result:

A lot of deja vu. In all fairness part of me did want to know why the pictures were all in the same spot. What else was in her house she was trying to hide? Satanic altar? Roommate orgy? A couch covered by a sheet? I'll never know.

Attempt #82
Mintcanteloupe

Background:

I had most definitely plumbed the depths of online dating. The only sin I had not yet committed was sending the same short message to every girl I found mildly attractive. I did not do this. I kept what dignity I had left, or at least as much dignity as a smart ass like me can muster.

The Message:

Wait, not to get too mired down in semantics, but if the first thing people notice about you is how high you can kick, does that mean that you're constantly walking around goose stepping or something along those lines? I'll be honest, if so, that seems a little weird. But I guess, who am I to judge? If that is your preferred method of movement, more power to ya. I just don't want to get accidentally kicked in the face if I ever meet you.

Well, with that out of the way, my name is Shawn, well rounded guy on okcupid, big reader who's attempting to broaden his literary base from the Star Wars books of his youth, resident smart ass, and man with a plan. Hello.

The Result:

Victory! I got a message back. I sent a second. I got a second back. It went on this way for a while. We went on some dates and both enjoyed them. Things moved along. I quit sending out messages and later even deactivated my profile.

The Fourth Hiatus

There are times in life when things go your way. Where the stars just magically align and you're finally given an opportunity to really have a go at grabbing the brass ring of happiness while being thrown around by the carousel which is our world. Unfortunately, there are also times when no matter how hard you try, things just don't go your way. This time was neither of those. Nope, this time was an utter and complete fuck up of mammoth proportions of which I was entirely and solely responsible. There's not a lot I could say about the several months I dated Mintcanteloupe. All you need to know is it ended because I couldn't commit, and that afterwards I spent a fairly long period of time working on myself to ensure it didn't happen again.

Okay, yeah, I can see how that might be a bit vague. All right then. Here he we go. I ended up cheating on her. She was a wonderful woman and I completely fucked it up because instead of dealing with my shit, I had just been pushing it down deep into bottom drawer of the metaphorical dresser of my psyche. As a result, I hurt both her and myself, and spent the next nine months or so working on figuring out why I did what I did. I'm not someone who has experienced a lot of healthy relationships, so when I finally found myself in one my subconscious freaked out pretty bad. Perhaps this darkens the tone of this collection a bit, you now knowing such things, but it is what it was, and such is life. Time heals all things, and making a mistake does not make one unlovable. With that in mind, I made a New Years resolution to get myself back out there, soon after reactivating and updating my profile.

Attempt #83
WombatsaurusRex

Background:

I didn't know what I was doing. What kind of message should I send? How should I do it? I was nervous, unsure. I decided to just dip my toe in the water. WombatsaurusRex's profile was pretty ho-hum, except for one strange mysterious reference.

The Message:

Wait.........what the hell is a pickle matrix?

The Result:

The lack of response was no surprise, but I still want to know what the hell a pickle matrix is. What could it be?

A Reversal of Roles

I'm not sure why, perhaps it was just me, but it seemed pretty rare for a woman to send a man an initial message back in the old days of the early 2010s. As I said, perhaps it was just me. Either way, it was not until this point that I got an initial message from a woman. I can't remember her profile name, so let's just call her Plymouth Voyager, because that's the kind of car she drove.

Plymouth Voyager first contacted me not long after I got back into online dating, and it must have been a fairly good message, or I just found her attractive, because I messaged her back, which must have been an all right response, because we messaged back and forth for awhile and then setup a date. The first date went fairly well, so we decided to go on a second, but this is where things began to go amiss in a way that I can only describe as apparently the norm for my life.

Now it's a well known fact that many women send texts to their friends after a date to summarize what happened. You know, things along the lines of:

Seems nice, but not all that into him. I could tell he wanted to kiss me but he didn't try to. Probably will go on a third date. Here's to settling. Hahaha.

Now imagine if that message, instead of getting sent to the intended recipient, instead gets sent to the guy from the date. Such is my life. To be fair to her, she quickly realized her mistake and profusely apologized, but then she also offered to have me hang out with her and her friends, which I politely declined, because why in the hell would anybody want to do that?

Attempt #84
Fancyraygun

Background:

Someone once told me that they got a message like the one below and thought it was extremely clever and instantly made them want to reply. Pretty good considering the huge influx of ab pics and short messages most women get on while online dating. Though I usually try to not copy the ideas of others, I decided I might as well give it a try. As they say, all is fair in love and war.

The Message:

Hello,
Funny, but still classy opening pick up line. Observation that I found your profile interesting. Statement that proves I read your profile, lets say note about Star Wars and the Great Gatsby. Comment with examples of how I have similar interests. Humorous remark about myself with just the right amount of self-deprecation to avoid looking cocky. Slightly risque observation. Closing that implies I hope to hear back from you.

The Result:

An important lesson in the world of online dating is you should never, ever, never copy someone else's strategy for initial messages. Be true to yourself. Unless you're just sending a bunch of ab pics or short messages. In that case, go to hell to you lazy skeezy bastard.

Attempt #85
DelightedlySloane

Background:

DelightedlySloane was an extremely good looking woman. Her profile was also fairly short with just a few little things here and there standing out. Apparently, she was just good looking enough where she didn't need much else. Not trying to bash her for it given it obviously worked for me.

The Message:

Hello Sloane. I'm assuming that's your name, though granted, you might just be a huge Ferris Bueller fan. Either way, I'm just going to go ahead and call you Sloane for now.

Anyways Sloane, I was perusing OKCupid and happened upon your profile. After giving it a read I have to say, I know it's been six years, but I'm still terribly disappointed that Flight of the Conchords never had a third season. There was only one show on television that combined dry wit and goofy songs, and I need it back. Now I have to makeup my own songs, and they just never work quite as well. Plus none of my friends or co-workers will join in when I start singing them.

Hope your having a good week.

Shawn

P.S. Don't worry. That's my actual name. At least I'm pretty sure it is. There is always the off chance that my parents have been lying to me for 32 years.

The Result:

For the record, I heard nothing back. However, as a slightly related fun fact, according to a fan theory the entire plot of *Ferris Bueller's Day Off* was the dorky kid imagining what his life would be like if he was cool, hence the girlfriend character, Sloane, was not real. So maybe in this case this Sloane wasn't real either. As a more important note for the record, *Flight of the Conchords* was an awesome show and they need to bring it back.

Attempt #86
PDXflowers

Background:

You would not believe the number of women who quote their score from the Myers Briggs personality quiz on their profiles. Apparently, a sizable group of people are convinced that an outdated and disproven personality quiz is the best way to decide with whom to copulate. PDXflowers hated the Myers-Briggs about as much as I did. She also claimed she was good with houseplants and was okay with peeing outside. It felt like she might be a good fit.

The Message:

I'm with you on the Myers Briggs score. To quote Thomas Jefferson:

"Fuck Myers Briggs."

Kudos for keeping houseplants alive. I have had the same house plant for the past twelve years. His name is Morton. He is the shit.

Also kudos for peeing outside. Nothing ruins a road trip more than having to stop at every damn gas station for a pee break. Need to pee? Here's a Gatorade bottle and funnel. This is no time to stop. We're adventuring. Don't think I care? Think about this. I didn't have to give you the funnel.

That's all I got for now.

The Result:

Maybe my stance on peeing while on road trips was a little too strong. Though maybe it was too weak and she was disgusted with me for being a pansy by offering her a funnel. Either way, no message back. On a more positive note, Morton is still alive and thriving today.

Attempt #87
Swedishgem

Background:

Let's be honest with ourselves. Everyone spices up their profiles a bit. It's natural, you want to put your best foot forward, but there are limits. You still have to stay within the realm of believability.

The Message:

I don't want to call BS on your photo captions, but I have a hard time believing your typical Sunday is you baking cakes in a gold sequin dress. I guess you could be going to a church bake sale or something along those lines every Sunday. But that seems a bit strange for an agnostic. However, if this is the case, kudos to you for wearing that dress even though it probably makes the old ladies in the front pews mutter things along the lines of "my goodness" and "I never".

The Result:

Nada. Though let's be honest with ourselves again, if your initial message is just calling out someone on their bullshit, they probably won't really want to message you back. Even if you bring up a very good point.

Attempt #88
Dorian_Grayest

Background:

Dorian_Grayests' profile mentioned that she had narrated some audio books. Thanks to a little adventure in high school this gave me the perfect in. A chance to show that we had something in common.

The Message:

So, true story. When I was in high school a local Vietnam vet wrote a book about his experiences in Vietnam which was actually pretty good. He than started on the dream of self-publishing, which back in 2000 was fairly forward thinking. As part of it he decided he wanted to do an audio version. For whatever reason, he chose me to do it. It never amounted to much, I think he ended up selling maybe thirty mp3's and my Mom refused to listen to it because it freaked her out to hear her son's voice talk about war. Such is my own limited foray into audio book narrating.

The Result:

Nope. Nothing back. Maybe she was looking for the whole opposites attract kind of thing. On a side note, if you'd be interested in hearing that audio book, I think I still have a copy lying around somewhere.

Attempt #89
Illa07

Background:

You'd think at some point I would know better, but apparently not. For those of you with good memories, you'll remember that I had messaged Illa07 before. For those of you who don't have good memories, she was Attempt #40. I apparently belong to the latter group given I did not realize this until I decided to send her a message. Discovering this, I had to decide whether or not to send her another message. Apparently, her profile was enticing enough that I decided going for it was the better decision.

The Message:

Well crap, looks like I tried to message you once before the last time I was on this thing. This is a first for me. Not really sure what to do. Screw it. Probably no harm in sending this message.

Hello. I was just perusing profiles and yours caught my eye. To be frank, part of it is that your a tall woman. Being a tall man its easier to dance with a tall woman. However, that's not the reason I'm sending this message. I'm sending this message because your profile suggests you'd be an interesting person to get to know, and I'd like a chance to do that. Past me seemed to think so, and present me agrees.

The Result:

Yeah, I’m not sure why I ever thought sending multiple initial messages to the same person would work. I’m also not sure why I felt the need to lie and say I never had sent multiple messages before. Perhaps regarding the latter, I didn’t want to seem weird, or you know, any weirder than a guy is when he sends multiple messages.

Attempt #90
Misakicupcakes

Background:

Things were starting to fall into their usual stride. I was spending way more time than I should coming up with messages that likely would never get answered. However, if there is one thing I am, it's stubborn. So, I soldiered on. This is a good way to look at life. Unfortunately, it can also lead to overly snarky messages.

The Message:

I was willing to believe that you were not actually a 74 year old woman, but then I realized that all of your favorite board games were ones that I have only ever played at my grandmother's house. On the plus side, my grandmother was an awesome person to hang out with, so I'd say sending this message is worth the risk.

That being said, I don't believe that you can only eat one chip. No one can eat only one chip. No one.

My name is Shawn by the way.

The Result:

Pro tip. Even if your grandmother was awesome, nobody in their late twenties or early thirties wants to be compared to her. Seriously. Don't do that. Also, no one can eat only one chip. No one.

Attempt #91
Stormi78

Background:

Stormi78's profile was a little ho-hum. About the only thing of interest was that she made the best brownies in the world. I found this to be a little grandiose of a claim, so I thought I'd set the record straight.

The Message:

How dare you. Everyone knows that Benito Mussolini made the best brownies in the world. This is certified by the International Brownie Symposium. You can find it on their website. He also invented that special brownie pan you can buy in Sky Mall where all the pieces are edge pieces. Trust me on that one, don't bother looking it up.

Now granted, you might make the best brownies in the world, when not including fascist dictators, and/or people who are dead, but I'd have to try one to be sure. I'll have to warn you though, I've eaten a lot of delicious brownies in my day.

The Result:

Another pro tip. Romance and made-up facts about fascist dictators rarely mix. Neither does insinuating that someone's brownies are not as good as they think they are. That's more of a second date kind of conversation.

Attempt #92
Brisk225

Background:

Things weren't going well on the old online dating front. Not a single response since I had gotten back into it, and I was starting to get a little desperate. Brisk225's profile didn't have a lot to it. The classic cute girl with "fun facts" that weren't really all that interesting and a plethora of travel pictures.

The Message:

Hi. Just perusing the old OkCupid and your profile caught my eye. As a fellow shameful snooze button abuser I can fully understand how you feel. Every time I swear that this time will be the last time, but nope it is not. Some day I'll just pop straight out of bed. Some day.

My name is Shawn by the way.

The Result:

Nothing back, but then again, I'm not sure I really wanted to hear anything back anyways. If your biggest fun fact is that you are a heavy abuser of the snooze button, you might not be that interesting.

Attempt #93
Plumgrey

Background:

If you can't tell, I was starting to get a little frustrated by this point. Why the hell put in any time if I never got anything back? Might as well just pick out a few things, mention them, and see what happens.

The Message:

Nice Freda costume.

By any chance in your first picture is that Mont St Michel int he background?

The Result:

Nope. Nothing. I'm kind of glad though. I'm pretty sure responding to a message like the one I had sent counts as a red flag.

Attempt #94
GratefulUnicorn

Background:

Okay. It was time to take a step back and rethink my strategies. Maybe I needed to be more straightforward. More direct. You know, still have a little humor, but try to be some kind of serious adult.

The Message:

Hi Heather, my name is Shawn. You seem like an intelligent woman with a good sense of humor, and I am interested in getting to know you.

I also like looking for the symbolism in my dreams, just for fun, but this one completely blew me away, what do you think?

The other night I dreamt that I went to a baseball game with my cousin Brian, college friend Dusty, and some guy that I sorta knew in high school. We all wore some kind of helmets that recorded everything we looked at. After the baseball game we stopped at a gas station and filled the car, but then discovered none of us had any money or cards. Luckily my Uncle Brian happened by with a puffin under his arm and paid for the gas.

Cheers.

The Result:

This is a road that I've gone down too many times before. Being serious doesn't work. Though then again, maybe whatever the hell my dream meant really freaked her out. Who knows?

Attempt #95
CMC929

Background:

CMC929's profile mentioned that she was looking for a partner in crime. This wasn't the first time I'd seen a comment like this, and part of me thought about reusing the same message from Attempt #64, but luckily I didn't let myself. Instead, I let the creative juices flow.

The Message:

Looking for a partner in crime eh. Well that's perfect, because I've been looking for one myself. I have a plan that's fool proof and sure to net us a couple hundred dollars....each.

The plan is we will go and rob the Goodwill in Sellwood. I'm pretty sure no one would ever see it coming so the police probably won't even respond. We won't grab money, we'll just grab as much old vintage clothing we can snag in under thirty seconds. Sellwood is a ritzy neighborhood full of old people so we're sure to net some awesome swag. We'll then drive to another Goodwill, and donate the clothes, earning us a healthy tax deduction for donations.

One of us needs to steal a getaway car, I say we just grab the nearest Car 2 Go. The other one needs to spray paint some squirt guns black. Don't use super soakers, the big tank is a dead giveaway.

You in?

The Result:

Apparently, she was only looking for a partner in very minor crimes. Not me, I'm ready for the big time. Time to collect those Benjamins. If any of you intrepid readers want in, let me know.

On a side note, Car2Go was a really cool service created in the middle of the second tech boom where you could rent a small two seated car with an app and park it wherever the hell you wanted. It was a pretty neat idea, but obviously didn't make any money, relying instead on constant inflow of venture capital to survive, an issue faced by most big tech ideas of the era. However, for some strange reason the heads of the company thought the answer to their money woes was to replace all the small two seaters with large Mercedes. The company went under not long after.

Attempt #96
Slvrnmph

Background:

I can’t even remember what in Slvrnmph’s profile sparked this weird thought in my head. Also, apparently I kind of got caught up on the whole Car2Go thing for a little bit around this time. What can I say? Weird times.

The Message:

I would usually call myself a fairly level headed individual, so such mischievous flights of fancy don't usually take root. However, I seem to have this growing need to spend a day renting as many Car 2 Go's as possible and parking them all in shady neighborhoods. I don't know why. I really have nothing against the whole concept of Car 2 Go. It's just something that sits in the back of my mind.

Anyway, that's a little random, but probably a pretty fair example of how my mind works. Responsible adult who sometimes gets weird ideas. My name is Shawn. Nice to meet you.

The Result:

I'm running out of synonyms for the word no. With my luck she was probably an avid Car2Go user who didn't think my plan to abuse the system was funny at all. Oh well, such is life.

It's probably worth mentioning that this was just one of my many ideas of ways to abuse the whole Car2Go thing. Others included seeing how many of the little buggers I could tip over, using them in a miniature road warrioresque game of tag, and having a contest to see how many someone could get parked in their neighborhood in a certain period of time.

Attempt #97
Royvin23

Background:

How far should you go for a joke? Should you maybe bend the truth a bit? Sure you might say, why not? But wait, others might say, if you might date someone shouldn't you always be honest? Beats me. All I know is that I was getting desperate.

The Message:

Pardon my French, but I fucking love pizza and wine. Just the other day I was having some pizza and wine. It was terrible pizza, but there was a large amount of wine, so I didn't even notice. Don't get me wrong, usually I try to go for higher quality pizza and wine, none of that Tostino's and Carlo Rossi for this man, but sometimes you just have to make the most you can out of what you have.

My name is Shawn by the way. Hello.

The Result:

It worked. It was blunt, a little over the top, and a bit of a lie (I like pizza and wine, but don't really love them), but it worked. A couple of messages back and forth, a date, but that was it. I didn't feel a connection and I didn't feel like continuing. She was nice, maybe too nice. The kind of nice where you wonder if they're secretly up to something. It was good to have one of these initial messages actually go somewhere though.

Attempt #98
PoodleParty

Background:

Hot off my first online dating success in god only knows how long, I hit the profiles again and went back to fishing. After perusing a bit, I found one that seemed to be interesting and launched out the wit.

The Message:

Oh sorry, honorary nativehood in Oregon doesn't take effect until 10 years. If it was me I'd say you've been here long enough, but you know how those bureaucrats are with their rules.

Given that we both hit the like button on this thing, it seems like maybe we can cut through a bit of the bullshit here. My name is Shawn. From your profile you seem like someone I'd be interested in meeting. Would you be interested in getting a coffee or beer sometime?

P.S. Nice Sisyphus reference in your "What I'm Doing With My Life." The East of Eden also caught my eye, of late I've been reading my way through Steinbeck.

The Result:

The message worked. A couple messages followed and before you know it, I was on a date. We talked about a lot of random things, which was not unenjoyable, but eventually it dawned on me that what I at first took to be joking around were signs of a more serious problem. The conversation jumped from one unrelated topic to the next, shifting without warning and without a clutch. She spoke in a rapid and manic manner, her eyes unable to focus on anything for long. It became worse as the date progressed, until finally I politely told her I had to go, paid for the beers we had ordered, and made my exit.

Conclusion

It was at this point that I quit online dating again, deactivating my profile and never returning to it. There were a lot of reasons why I quit. One was the experience with PoodleParty. I'm not sure if I can really explain it, but the date with her had made me uneasy in a way I had not experienced before through all my misadventures in online dating. In retrospect, she had shown many red flags, but they had all been ignored by my desperation to meet somebody. The other reason was I did not like the kind of person I was becoming. The significant number of rejections by people I had never met was beginning to make me bitter in ways that I didn't like. Both of these combined made it seem best to move on.

It would be several years later before I bothered with online dating again. By then things had changed. The old websites with their ridiculous amounts of personal information were quickly losing their relevance to the rising dominance of the swiping apps. Replaced by a model involving representing oneself with a couple of blurbs and photos, easily digestible and judgeable. The experience of finding a prospective mate was boiled down to its most basic principles, commodified and gamified for the purpose of keeping people looking, and therefore still using the apps, rather than helping them find someone to love. It was the end of an era, and the beginning of the end for the art of crafting the perfect initial message. In the end, those who treated finding prospective mates like an assembly line won the day, and today it seems if an initial message is over a sentence, it's considered weird. So it goes.

I guess some of you were probably hoping for a better ending than this one. Maybe some of you were hoping for some kind of happy ending where I found the one, attracting her with the perfect initial message, or at least a situation where I learned some kind of profound lesson about myself that maybe some of you could use in your own lives. Unfortunately, this ends with neither one of those. It just ends. I'm not sure of any definitive way one is supposed to meet someone, I don't have any secrets to share, and if I learned anything it was unrelated to the initial messages I sent out. So it goes.

All right, I can see that some of you probably aren't all that happy about this book ending with a swift closing of the door. Some of you are old school and need a reason to read something beyond a few laughs along the way. You need growth. You need change. Okay then. How about don't be surprised when you catch the type of fish for which you bait your hook? Not good enough? Hmmm. What about, be yourself or else you will have to pretend to be someone else your entire life? Maybe, but I think I can do better. How about this? We are all just a bunch of hyper-intelligent apes living by made up rules on a tiny speck of sand circling an insignificant yellow sun, so we might as well be kind to each other and help each other laugh. Be open to the world. Embrace it. That seems good enough. So it goes.

Also Written By The Author

The Uncanny Valley

We all know a Paul. A person who seems to see stuff that isn't there. The type the polite call quirky and the blunt call nuts. Conspiracies? He's got a few. He's got his finger on how the world really works. He knows what kind of shit is coming down the pipe. Flee across the West Texas desert to Mexico? Makes sense to him. Feel like you're being watched? You bet your ass someone is watching. Best turn off your cellphone. Troubles? Of course, that's just part of life. Doubts? No time for doubts. Shit is getting real. Get in, buckle up, crack open a beer. The only real question is, how far down the rabbit hole are you willing to follow?

An Unsated Thirst

They say that an author's first stories are their most raw. Here is a collection of S.W. Campbell's first short stories and writings. Combining both published and unpublished works, An Unsated Thirst explores victory and defeat, triumph and shame, and an unflinching view of our naked selves. How one views such stories is dependent upon the mood of the reader. Whether we are at our highs or at our lows. However, it is hard for any of us to claim that such stories are ones that we cannot identify with. Contained within these pages are parts of our lives which we try to forget, though they are an important part of what makes us whole. Such stories should be embraced, accepted within ourselves so we can better accept them with others.

Papaya

When a devastating hurricane hits the Caribbean island of Domenique, its inhabitants are forced into a singular struggle to survive and rebuild. Isolated in their midst is Ted, a Peace Corps volunteer who fled the ashes of his former life only to find himself labeled an outsider. Infatuated by the enigmatic wife of his only friend, Ted thrusts himself into a world beyond his comprehension. As obsession turns to desperation, tensions grow and Ted is forced to decide exactly how far he will go to rebuild amidst the muddy ruins.

Stumptown

There are places where people say things are better. Where the downtowns do not empty after dark and people dare to dream beyond their means. Quirky utopias where the sins of the past are washed away by gentle rains and we all go forward arm in arm together into the brightening sunshine. Distant locations flocked to by young pilgrims, unencumbered by the deeply driven roots of age, where everything will be different. Combining both published and unpublished work, Stumptown is a collection of stories about ordinary people, navigating their personal anxieties and drama in a time when uncertainties were still tucked away and not allowed to distort the sense of hope in the air. It is a soliloquy to naivete, and the belief that a better world is a place rather than an idea.

The People's Republic of 47th & Long

Perhaps the world would be a better place if we thought of ourselves less as good people, and more as lousy people who manage to do good things. My friend Leopold was always a dreamer. The pandemic and our reactions to it left us broken and divided. Most of us just wanted to feel safe again, but others dreamt of something better. Leopold was one of these. Though I think he likely joined the People's Republic of 47th and Long purely out of geographic convenience, I know once part of it, he fully shared in its egalitarian vision. All I have are his letters. Sometimes I wish I had burned them, but I didn't, so now here they are. Maybe you can find a use for them. Perhaps they can help remind you who we truly are. The good, the bad, and most importantly, the indifferent.

The Man In The Sodden Cap

The Man In The Sodden Cap is a collection of twenty-six short stories written during a period of emotional unleashing, a madcap rush to get words to the page. As with any such period of unrelenting literary expulsion, the results are a mix of emotional, personal, poignant, and inane. For many authors, these are the types of stories that often get kept in a drawer somewhere, not shared with anyone. But what use are stories if they are not shared? Individually these are good stories, but taken all together they tell the tale of heartbreak and remorse, and the need to move on. In this context, The Man In A Sodden Cap is in many ways a sequel to S.W. Campbell's first short story collection, An Unsated Thirst, a continuation and fitting conclusion to that earlier work.

Senseless Sensibilities

It is the human condition to try and find meaning in this life, to make sense of the chaos and randomness around us. At times this need overwhelms common sense, building layers of cognitive dissonance until we are left running our lives based upon senseless sensibilities. Contained within these pages are thirty-six short stories which explore the ability of people to adapt and survive the world around them. Stories which provide insight into slices of existence, and which highlight the strange ridiculousness of everyday life. Whether it's an old man adapting his hobbies to his aging body, a commodities trader who finds himself to be the commodity, or a lonely man fulfilling two needs in a single cross-country trip, each shows the resilience and mental flexibility shared by us all.

More information can be found at:

www.shawnwcampbell.com

About The Author

S.W. Campbell was born in Eastern Oregon in 1983 after a harrowing drive through a fog. He currently resides in Portland, Oregon where he works as an economist and lives with a lovely house plant named Morton. He has had many short stories published in various literary reviews, some of which appear in this work, and has also self-published several books. His work can be found at www.shawnwcampbell.com.

www.ingramcontent.com/pod-product-compliance
Lightning Source LLC
Chambersburg PA
CBHW072343090426
42741CB00012B/2900

* 9 7 9 8 9 8 7 0 2 8 7 4 2 *